BRITISH RAILWAYS ~~BOO~~

COA
ST

THIRTIETH EDITION
2006

The complete guide to all
Locomotive-Hauled Coaches which
operate on National Rail

Peter Hall & Peter Fox

PLATFORM
5

ISBN 1 902336 46 1

© 2005. Platform 5 Publishing Ltd., 3 Wyvern House, Sark Road, Sheffield, S2 4HG, England.

CONTENTS

PROVISION OF INFORMATION

This book has been compiled with care to be as accurate as possible, but in some cases official information is not available and the publisher cannot be held responsible for any errors or omissions. We would like to thank the companies and individuals which have been co-operative in supplying information to us. The authors of this series of books will be pleased to receive notification from readers of any inaccuracies readers may find in the series, and notification of any additional information to supplement our records and thus enhance future editions is always welcome. Please send comments to:

Robert Pritchard, Platform 5 Publishing Ltd., 3 Wyvern House, Sark Road, Sheffield, S2 4HG, England.

Tel: 0114 255 2625   **Fax:** 0114 255 2471   **e-mail:** robert@platform5.com

This book is updated to 15 August 2005.

UPDATES

This book is updated to the Stock Changes given in **entrain 46** (October 2005). Readers are therefore advised to update this book from the official Platform 5 Stock Changes published every month in **entrain**, starting with issue 47.

For further details of **entrain**, please see the advertisement on the back cover of this book.

BRITAIN'S RAILWAY SYSTEM

INFRASTRUCTURE & OPERATION

Britain's national railway infrastructure is now owned by a "not for dividend" company, Network Rail. Many stations and maintenance depots are leased to and operated by Train Operating Companies (TOCs), but some larger stations remain under Network Rail control. The only exception is the infrastructure on the Isle of Wight, which is nationally owned and is leased to the Island Line franchisee.

Trains are operated by TOCs over Network Rail, regulated by access agreements between the parties involved. In general, TOCs are responsible for the provision and maintenance of the locomotives, rolling stock and staff necessary for the direct operation of services, whilst Network Rail is responsible for the provision and maintenance of the infrastructure and also for staff needed to regulate the operation of services.

DOMESTIC PASSENGER TRAIN OPERATORS

The large majority of passenger trains are operated by the TOCs on fixed term franchises. Franchise expiry dates are shown in parentheses in the list of franchisees below:

Franchise	Franchisee	Trading Name
Central Trains[1]	National Express Group plc (until 1 April 2006)	Central Trains
Chiltern Railways	M40 Trains Ltd. (until December 2021)	Chiltern Railways
Cross-Country[2]	Virgin Rail Group Ltd. (until further notice)	Virgin Trains
Gatwick Express[3]	National Express Group plc (until 27 April 2011)	Gatwick Express
Great Western Trains[4]	First Group plc (until 31 March 2006)	First Great Western
Greater Anglia[5]	National Express Group plc (until 31 March 2014)	London Eastern Railway ("One")
InterCity East Coast[6]	GNER Holdings plc (until 30 April 2012)	Great North Eastern Railway
InterCity West Coast	Virgin Rail Group Ltd. (until 8 March 2012)	Virgin Trains
Island Line	Stagecoach Holdings plc (until February 2007)	Island Line
LTS Rail	National Express Group plc (until 25 May 2011)	c2c
Merseyrail Electrics[7]	Serco/NedRail (until 20 July 2028)	Merseyrail Electrics

Midland Main Line	National Express Group plc (until 27 April 2008)	Midland Mainline
North London Railways	National Express Group plc (until 17 October 2006)	Silverlink Train Services
Northern Rail[8]	Serco/NedRail (until 11 September 2013)	Northern
ScotRail	First Group plc (until 16 October 2011)	First ScotRail
South Central	GoVia Ltd. (Go-Ahead/Keolis). (until May 2010)	Southern
South Eastern[9]		South Eastern Trains
South Western	Stagecoach Holdings plc (until 3 February 2007)	South West Trains
Thames[4]	First Group plc (until 31 March 2006)	First Great Western Link
Thameslink	GoVia Ltd. (until 1 April 2006)	Thameslink Rail
Trans-Pennine Express	First Group/Keolis (until 31 January 2012)	First Trans-Pennine Express
Wales & Borders	Arriva Trains Ltd (until 6 December 2018)	Arriva Trains Wales
Wessex Trains[4]	National Express Group plc (until 31 March 2006)	Wessex Trains
Great Northern[10]	National Express Group plc (until 4 April 2006)	WAGN

Notes:

[1] Due to be abolished on expiry. Services expected to be split between Chiltern, Midland Mainline, Northern, "One", Silverlink, Trans-Pennine Express and Cross-Country. The current Central Trains franchise is now expected to continue until the end of 2006 but no official decision had been made at the time of going to press.

[2] At the time of going to press the future of this franchise was in doubt following its renegotiation, as the Strategic Rail Authority (SRA) then announced that Virgin's best and final offer for a single-tender deal running until 2012 did not represent value for money. The SRA has therefore told Virgin that it reserves the right to terminate the franchise.

[3] Gatwick Express has been proposed for possible absorption by Southern as part of the SRA's Brighton Main Line Route Utilisation Strategy. This could take place before the expiry of the current Gatwick Express franchise.

[4] Due to transfer to the new Greater Western franchise on 1 April 2006.

[5] Incorporates the former Anglia and Great Eastern franchises and the West Anglia half of West Anglia Great Northern. Awarded for seven years with a likely extension for a further three.

[6] The new East Coast franchise started on 1 May 2005 for seven years, to be extended by a further three if performance targets are met.

[7] Now under control of Merseyrail PTE instead of the SRA. Franchise due to be reviewed after seven years and then every five years to fit in with

Merseyside Local Transport Plan.

[8] Urban and rural services previously run by Arriva Trains Northern and First North Western were transferred to the new Northern franchise on 12 December 2004. Trans-Pennine services formerly run by these operators were taken over by the new Trans-Pennine Express franchise on 1 February 2004. The Northern franchise runs for up to 8¾ years.

[9] New interim management company known as South Eastern Trains (SET) formed on 9 November 2003, pending award of new Integrated Kent franchise expected in the latter part of 2005. SET is a subsidiary of the SRA.

[10] The West Anglia half of WAGN transferred to new Greater Anglia franchise. The Great Northern half remains separate until its absorption by the new Thameslink franchise in 2006. Despite this, Great Northern continues to use the brand name WAGN and has said it now wishes to be referred to as "W-A-G-N", not as WAGN.

A major reorganisation of franchises is under way. See **entrain** for developments.

The following operators run non-franchised services only:

Operator	Trading Name	Route
British Airports Authority	Heathrow Express	London Paddington–Heathrow Airport
Hull Trains§	Hull Trains	London King's Cross–Hull
West Coast Railway Co.	West Coast Railway	Birmingham Snow Hill–Stratford-on-Avon
		Fort William–Mallaig*
		York–Scarborough*

* Special summer-dated services only.
§ Now owned by First Group.

INTERNATIONAL PASSENGER OPERATIONS

Eurostar (UK) operates international passenger-only services between the United Kingdom and continental Europe, jointly with French National Railways (SNCF) and Belgian National Railways (SNCB/NMBS). Eurostar (UK) is a subsidiary of London & Continental Railways, which is jointly owned by National Express Group plc and British Airways.

In addition, a service for the conveyance of accompanied road vehicles through the Channel Tunnel is provided by the tunnel operating company, Eurotunnel.

FREIGHT TRAIN OPERATIONS

The following operators are licensed to operate freight train services:

Cotswold Rail Engineering.*
Direct Rail Services Ltd.
English Welsh & Scottish Railway Ltd (EWS).
Freightliner Ltd.
FM Rail.*
GB Railfreight Ltd. (now owned by First Group)
West Coast Railway Co.*
(*Licence obtained but only empty coaching stock trains operated at present).

INTRODUCTION

LAYOUT OF INFORMATION

Coaches are listed in numerical order of painted number in batches according to type.

Each coach entry is laid out as in the following example (former number column may be omitted where not applicable):

No.	Prev. No.	Notes	Livery	Owner	Operator	Depot/Location
42348	(41073)	*	**FG**	A	*GW*	LA

Note that the operator is the organisation which facilitates the use of the coach and may not be the actual train operating company which runs the train. For example coaches operated by Riviera Trains might run in trains which are operated by Arriva Trains Wales.

DETAILED INFORMATION & CODES

Under each type heading, the following details are shown:

* 'Mark' of coach (see below).
* Descriptive text.
* Number of first class seats, standard class seats, lavatory compartments and wheelchair spaces shown as F/S nT nW respectively.
* Bogie type (see below).
* Additional features.
* ETH Index.

TOPS TYPE CODES

TOPS type codes are allocated to all coaching stock. For vehicles numbered in the passenger stock number series the code consists of:

(1) Two letters denoting the layout of the vehicle as follows:

AA	Gangwayed Corridor
AB	Gangwayed Corridor Brake
AC	Gangwayed Open (2+2 seating)
AD	Gangwayed Open (2+1 seating)
AE	Gangwayed Open Brake
AF	Gangwayed Driving Open Brake
AG	Micro-Buffet
AH	Brake Micro-Buffet
AI	As 'AC' but with drop-head buckeye and gangway at one end only
AJ	Restaurant Buffet with Kitchen
AK	Kitchen Car
AL	As 'AC' but with disabled person's toilet (Mark 4 only)
AN	Miniature Buffet
AP	Pullman First with Kitchen

AQ Pullman Parlour First
AR Pullman Brake First
AS Sleeping Car
AT Royal Train Coach
AU Sleeping Car with Pantry
AV Mark 4 Barrier Vehicle
AW EMU Translator vehicle
AX Generator Van (1000 V DC)
AZ Special Saloon
GS HST Barrier Vehicle
NW Desiro Barrier Vehicle

(2) A digit denoting the class of passenger accommodation:

1	First	4 Unclassified
2	Standard (formerly second)	5 None
3	Composite (first & standard)	

(3) A suffix relating to the build of coach.

1	Mark 1	C	Mark 2C	G	Mark 3 or 3A
Z	Mark 2	D	Mark 2D	H	Mark 3B
A	Mark 2A	E	Mark 2E	J	Mark 4
B	Mark 2B	F	Mark 2F		

OPERATING CODES

Operating codes used by train company operating staff (and others) to denote vehicle types in general. These are shown in parentheses adjacent to TOPS type codes. Letters used are:

B Brake	K Side corridor with lavatory
C Composite	O Open
F First Class	S Standard Class (formerly second)

Various other letters are in use and the meaning of these can be ascertained by referring to the titles at the head of each type.

Readers should note the distinction between an SO (Open Standard) and a TSO (Tourist Open Standard) The former has 2+1 seating layout, whilst the latter has 2+2.

BOGIE TYPES

BR Mark 1 (BR1). Double bolster leaf spring bogie. Generally 90 m.p.h., but Mark 1 bogies may be permitted to run at 100 m.p.h. with special maintenance. Weight: 6.1 t.

BR Mark 2 (BR2). Single bolster leaf-spring bogie used on certain types of non-passenger stock and suburban stock (all now withdrawn). Weight: 5.3 t.

COMMONWEALTH (C). Heavy, cast steel coil spring bogie. 100 m.p.h. Weight: 6.75 t.

B4. Coil spring fabricated bogie. Generally 100 m.p.h., but B4 bogies may be permitted to run at 110 m.p.h. with special maintenance. Weight: 5.2 t.

B5. Heavy duty version of B4. 100 m.p.h. Weight: 5.3 t.
B5 (SR). A bogie originally used on Southern Region EMUs, similar in design to B5. Now also used on locomotive hauled coaches. 100 m.p.h.
BT10. A fabricated bogie designed for 125 m.p.h. Air suspension.
T4. A 125 m.p.h. bogie designed by BREL (now Bombardier Transportation).
BT41. Fitted to Mark 4 vehicles, designed by SIG in Switzerland. At present limited to 125 m.p.h., but designed for 140 m.p.h.

BRAKES

Air braking is now standard on British main line trains. Vehicles with other equipment are denoted:

v   Vacuum braked.
x   Dual braked (air and vacuum).

HEATING & VENTILATION

Electric heating and ventilation is now standard on British main-line trains. Certain coaches for use on charter services may also have steam heating facilities, or be steam heated only.

PUBLIC ADDRESS

It is assumed all coaches are now fitted with public address equipment, although certain stored vehicles may not have this feature. In addition, it is assumed all vehicles with a conductor's compartment have public address transmission facilities, as have catering vehicles.

COOKING EQUIPMENT

It is assumed that Mark 1 catering vehicles have gas powered cooking equipment, whilst Mark 2, 3 and 4 catering vehicles have electric powered cooking equipment unless stated otherwise.

ADDITIONAL FEATURE CODES

d   Secondary door locking.
dg   Driver–Guard communication equipment.
f   Facelifted or fluorescent lighting.
k   Composition brake blocks (instead of cast iron).
n   Day/night lighting.
p   Public telephone.
pg   Public address transmission and driver-guard communication.
pt   Public address transmission facility.
q   Catering staff to shore telephone.
w   Wheelchair space.
z   Disabled persons' toilet.
★   Blue star multiple working cables fitted.

Standard class coaches with wheelchair space also have one tip-up seat per space.

NOTES ON ETH INDICES

The sum of ETH indices in a train must not be more than the ETH index of the locomotive. The normal voltage on British trains is 1000 V. Suffix 'X' denotes 600 amp wiring instead of 400 amp. Trains whose ETH index is higher than 66 must be formed completely of 600 amp wired stock. Class 33 and 73 locomotives cannot provide a suitable electric train supply for Mark 2D, Mark 2E, Mark 2F, Mark 3, Mark 3A, Mark 3B or Mark 4 coaches. Class 55 locomotives provide an e.t.s. directly from one of their traction generators into the train line. Consequently voltage fluctuations can result in motor-alternator flashover. Thus these locomotives are not suitable for use with Mark 2D, Mark 2E, Mark 2F, Mark 3, Mark 3A, Mark 3B or Mark 4 coaches unless modified motor-alternators are fitted. Such motor alternators were fitted to Mark 2D and 2F coaches used on the East Coast main line, but few remain fitted.

BUILD DETAILS

Lot Numbers
Vehicles ordered under the auspices of BR were allocated a lot (batch) number when ordered and these are quoted in class headings and sub-headings.

Builders
These are shown in class headings, the following designations being used:

Ashford	BR, Ashford Works.
BRCW	Birmingham Railway Carriage & Wagon Company., Smethwick, Birmingham.
BREL Derby	BREL, Derby Carriage Works (later ABB/Adtranz Derby, now Bombardier Derby).
Charles Roberts	Charles Roberts and Company., Horbury, Wakefield (now Bombardier Transportaion)
Cravens	Cravens, Sheffield.
Derby	BR, Derby Carriage Works (later BREL Derby, then ABB / Adtranz Derby, now Bombardier Derby).
Doncaster	BR, Doncaster Works (later BREL Doncaster, then BRML Doncaster, then ABB/Adtranz Doncaster, now Bombardier).
Eastleigh	BR, Eastleigh Works (later BREL Eastleigh, then Wessex Traincare, now Alstom Eastleigh).
Glasgow	BR Springburn Works, Glasgow (now Alstom, Glasgow)
Gloucester	The Gloucester Railway Carriage & Wagon Co.
Hunslet-Barclay	Hunslet Barclay, Kilmarnock Works
Metro-Cammell	Metropolitan-Cammell, Saltley, Birmingham (later GEC-Alsthom Birmingham, now Alstom Birmingham).
Pressed Steel	Pressed Steel, Linwood.
Swindon	BR Swindon Works
Wolverton	BR Wolverton Works (later BREL Wolverton then Railcare, Wolverton, now Alstom Wolverton).
York	BR, York Carriage Works (later BREL York, then ABB York).

Information on sub-contracting works which built parts of vehicles e.g. the underframes etc. is not shown.

In addition to the above, certain vintage Pullman cars were built or rebuilt at the following works:

Metropolitan Carriage & Wagon Company, Birmingham (Now Alstom)
Midland Carriage & Wagon Company, Birmingham
Pullman Car Company, Preston Park, Brighton
Conversions have also been carried out at the Railway Technical Centre, Derby, LNWR, Crewe and Blakes Fabrications, Edinburgh.

Vehicle Numbers

Where a coach has been renumbered, the former number is shown in parentheses. If a coach has been renumbered more than once, the original number is shown first in parentheses, followed by the most recent number. Where the former number of a coach due to be converted or renumbered is known and the conversion and/or renumbering has not yet taken place, the coach is listed under both current number (with depot allocation) and under new number (without allocation).

Numbering Systems

Seven different numbering systems were in use on BR. These were the BR series, the four pre-nationalisation companies' series', the Pullman Car Company's series and the UIC (International Union of Railways) series. BR number series coaches and former Pullman Car Company series are listed separately. There is also a separate listing of 'Saloon' type vehicles which are registered to run on National Rail. Please note the Mark 2 Pullman vehicles were ordered after the Pullman Car Company had been nationalised and are therefore numbered in the BR series.

THE DEVELOPMENT OF BR STANDARD COACHES

The standard BR coach built from 1951 to 1963 was the Mark 1. This type features a separate underframe and body. The underframe is normally 64 ft. 6 in. long, but certain vehicles were built on shorter (57 ft.) frames. Tungsten lighting was standard and until 1961, BR Mark 1 bogies were generally provided. In 1959 Lot No. 30525 (TSO) appeared with fluorescent lighting and melamine interior panels, and from 1961 onwards Commonwealth bogies were fitted in an attempt to improve the quality of ride which became very poor when the tyre profiles on the wheels of the BR1 bogies became worn. Later batches of TSO and BSO retained the features of Lot No. 30525, but compartment vehicles – whilst utilising melamine panelling in standard class – still retained tungsten lighting. Wooden interior finish was retained in first class vehicles where the only change was to fluorescent lighting in open vehicles (except Lot No. 30648, which had tungsten lighting). In later years many Mark 1 coaches had BR 1 bogies replaced by B4.

In 1964, a new prototype train was introduced. Known as 'XP64', it featured new seat designs, pressure heating & ventilation, aluminium compartment doors and corridor partitions, foot pedal operated toilets and B4 bogies. The vehicles were built on standard Mark 1 underframes. Folding exterior doors were fitted, but these proved troublesome and were later replaced with hinged doors. All XP64 coaches have been withdrawn, but some have been preserved. The prototype Mark 2 vehicle (W 13252) was produced in 1963. This was an FK of semi-integral construction and had pressure heating & ventilation, tungsten lighting, and was mounted on B4 bogies. This vehicle has been preserved by the National Railway Museum and is currently stored at MoD Kineton DM. The production build was similar, but wider windows were used. The TSO and SO vehicles used a new seat design similar to that in the XP64 and fluorescent lighting was provided. Interior finish reverted to wood. Mark 2 vehicles were built from 1964–66.

The Mark 2A design, built 1967–68, incorporated the remainder of the features first used in the XP64 coaches, i.e. foot pedal operated toilets (except BSO), new first class seat design, aluminium compartment doors and partitions together with fluorescent lighting in first class compartments. Folding gangway doors (lime green coloured) were used instead of the traditional one-piece variety.

The following list summarises the changes made in the later Mark 2 variants:

Mark 2B: Wide wrap around doors at vehicle ends, no centre doors, slightly longer body. In standard class, one toilet at each end instead of two at one end as previously. Red folding gangway doors.

Mark 2C: Lowered ceiling with twin strips of fluorescent lighting and ducting for air conditioning, but air conditioning not fitted.

Mark 2D: Air conditioning. No opening top-lights in windows.

Mark 2E: Smaller toilets with luggage racks opposite. Fawn folding gangway doors.

Mark 2F: Plastic interior panels. Inter-City 70 type seats. Modified air conditioning system.

The Mark 3 design has BT10 bogies, is 75 ft. (23 m.) long and is of fully integral construction with Inter-City 70 type seats. Gangway doors were yellow (red in RFB) when new, although these are being changed on refurbishment. Loco-hauled coaches are classified Mark 3A, Mark 3 being reserved for HST trailers. A new batch of FO and BFO, classified Mark 3B, was built in 1985 with Advanced Passenger Train-style seating and revised lighting. The last vehicles in the Mark 3 series were the driving brake vans built for West Coast Main Line services.

The Mark 4 design was built by Metro-Cammell for use on the East Coast Main Line after electrification and features a body profile suitable for tilting trains, although tilt is not fitted, and is not intended to be. This design is suitable for 140 m.p.h. running, although is restricted to 125 m.p.h. because the signalling system on the route is not suitable for the higher speed. The bogies for these coaches were built by SIG in Switzerland and are designated BT41. Power operated sliding plug exterior doors are standard. At the time of writing all but one set of these coaches and two spare vehicles had been rebuilt with completely new interiors and are referred to as "Mallard stock" by GNER

1. BR NUMBER SERIES STOCK
PASSENGER STOCK

AJ11 (RF)   RESTAURANT FIRST

Mark 1. Spent most of its life as a Royal Train vehicle and was numbered 2907 for a time. Built with Commonwealth bogies, but B5 bogies substituted. 24/–. ETH 2.

Lot No. 30633 Swindon 1961. 41 t.

| 325 | **PC** | VS | *VS* | SL | |

AP1Z (PFK)   PULLMAN FIRST WITH KITCHEN

Mark 2. Pressure Ventilated. Seating removed and replaced with servery. 2T. B5 bogies. ETH 6.

Lot No. 30755 Derby 1966. 40 t.

| 504 | **PC** | WC | *WC* | CS | ULLSWATER |
| 506 | **PC** | WC | *WC* | CS | WINDERMERE |

AQ1Z (PFP)   PULLMAN PARLOUR FIRST

Mark 2. Pressure Ventilated. 36/– 2T. B4 bogies. ETH 5.

Non-standard Livery: 546 is maroon & beige.

Lot No. 30754 Derby 1966. 35 t.

546	**0**	WC		CS	CITY OF MANCHESTER
548	**PC**	WC	*WC*	CS	GRASMERE
549	**PC**	WC	*WC*	CS	BASSENTHWAITE
550	**PC**	WC	*WC*	CS	RYDAL WATER
551	**PC**	WC	*WC*	CS	BUTTERMERE
552	**PC**	WC	*WC*	CS	ENNERDALE WATER
553	**PC**	WC	*WC*	CS	CRUMMOCK WATER

AR1Z (PFB)   PULLMAN BRAKE FIRST

Mark 2. Pressure Ventilated. 30/– 2T. B4 bogies. ETH 4.

Lot No. 30753 Derby 1966. 35 t.

| 586 | **PC** | WC | *WC* | CS | DERWENTWATER |

AJ21 (RG)   GRIDDLE CAR

Mark 1. Rebuilt from RF. –/30. B5 bogies. ETH 2.

This vehicle was numbered DB975878 for a time when in departmental service for British Railways.

Lot No. 30013 Doncaster 1952. Rebuilt Wolverton 1965. 40 t.

| 1105 | (302) | v | **G** | MH | *MH* | RL |

AJ1F (RFB)   BUFFET OPEN FIRST

Mark 2F. Air conditioned. Converted 1988–9/91 at BREL, Derby from Mark 2F
FOs. 1200/1/3/6/11/14–16/20/21/50/2/5/6/9 have Stones equipment, others have
Temperature Ltd. 25/– 1T 1W (except 1253 which is 26/– 1T). B4 bogies. d.
ETH 6X.

1200/3/6/11/14/16/20/52/5/6. Lot No. 30845 Derby 1973. 33 t.
1201/4/5/7/8/10/12/13/15/18/19/21/50/1/4/8/60. Lot No. 30859 Derby 1973–
74. 33 t.
1202/9/53/8. Lot No. 30873 Derby 1974–75. 33 t.

† Fitted with new m.a. sets.

1200	(3287, 6459)	†	**RV**	H	*RV*	CP
1201	(3361, 6445)		**V**	H		TM
1202	(3436, 6456)	†	**V**	H		KT
1203	(3291)	†		H	*RV*	CP
1204	(3401)	†	**V**	H		PY
1205	(3329, 6438)	†	**V**	AE		ZA
1206	(3319)	†	**V**	H		KT
1207	(3328, 6422)	†	**V**	H		KT
1208	(3393)		**V**	H		KT
1209	(3437, 6457)	†	**V**	H		ZH
1210	(3405, 6462)	†	**CP**	H	*SR*	IS
1211	(3305)			H	*FM*	OY
1212	(3427, 6453)	†	**V**	H	*RV*	CP
1213	(3419)	†	**V**	H		KT
1214	(3317, 6433)		**AR**	H	*1A*	NC
1215	(3377)		**AR**	H	*1A*	NC
1216	(3302)	†	**V**	H	*RV*	CP
1218	(3332)		**AR**	H	*1A*	NC
1219	(3418)		**AR**	H	*1A*	NC
1220	(3315, 6432)	†	**CS**	H	*SR*	IS
1221	(3371)			H	*FM*	OY
1250	(3372)	†	**V**	H	*RV*	CP
1251	(3383)	†	**V**	H		KT
1252	(3280)	†	**V**	H		KT
1253	(3432)	†	**V**	H		KT
1254	(3391)	†	**V**	H	*FM*	OY
1255	(3284)	†	**V**	H		KT
1256	(3296)	†		H	*FM*	OY
1258	(3322)	†	**V**	H	*RV*	CP
1259	(3439)	†	**V**	H		KT
1260	(3378)	†	**V**	H	*RV*	CP

AK51 (RKB)   KITCHEN BUFFET

Mark 1. No seats. B5 bogies. ETH 1.

Lot No. 30624 Cravens 1960–61. 41 t.

1566   **VN** VS *VS* CP

AJ41 (RBR)   RESTAURANT BUFFET

Mark 1. Built with 23 loose chairs. All remaining vehicles refurbished with 23 fixed polypropylene chairs and fluorescent lighting. ETH 2 (2X*). 1683/92/99 were further refurbished with 21 chairs, wheelchair space and carpets.

s Modified for use as servery vehicle with seating removed.

1646–1699. Lot No. 30628 Pressed Steel 1960–61. Commonwealth bogies. 39 t.
1730. Lot No. 30512 BRCW 1960–61. B5 bogies. 37 t.

Non-standard Livery: 1651, 1683 and 1699 are Oxford blue.

1646		FM		RD	1680	*s	**GC**	E	*E*	OM
1651	**O**	RV		CO	1683	s	**O**	RV	*RV*	CP
1657	**CH**	FM	*FM*	OY	1692	s	**CH**	RV	*RV*	CP
1658	**BG**	E	*E*	OM	1696		**G**	E	*E*	OM
1659	s	**PC**	RA	*WT*	OM	1698	s	**GC**	E	*E*	OM
1671	x*	**M**	E	*E*	OM	1699	s	**O**	RV	*RV*	CP
1679	s	**GC**	E	*E*	OM	1730	x	**M**	BK	*BK*	BT

AN2F (RSS)   SELF-SERVICE BUFFET CAR

Mark 2F. Air conditioned. Temperature Ltd. equipment. Inter-City 70 seats. Converted 1974 from a Mark 2F TSO as a prototype self-service buffet for APT-P. Sold to Northern Ireland Railways 1983 and regauged to 5'3". Since withdrawn, repatriated to Great Britain and converted back to standard gauge. –/24. B5 bogies. ETH 12X.

Lot No. 30860 Derby 1973–74. 33 t.

1800   (5970, NIR546)   **PC** WT *WT* OM

AN21 (RMB)   MINIATURE BUFFET CAR

Mark 1. –/44 2T. These vehicles are basically an open standard with two full window spaces removed to accommodate a buffet counter, and four seats removed to allow for a stock cupboard. All remaining vehicles now have fluorescent lighting. Commonwealth bogies. ETH 3.

1813–1832. Lot No. 30520 Wolverton 1960. 38 t.
1840–1842. Lot No. 30507 Wolverton 1960. 37 t.
1859–1863. Lot No. 30670 Wolverton 1961–62. 38 t.
1882. Lot No. 30702 Wolverton 1962. 38 t.

1842 is refurbished and fitted with a microwave oven.

1813	x	**M**	E	*E*	OM		1860	x	**M**	WC	*WC*	CS
1832	x	**G**	E	*E*	OM		1861	x	**M**	WC	*WC*	CS
1840	v	**G**	FM	*FM*	RL		1863	x	**CH**	RV	*RV*	CP
1842	x	**CH**	RV	*RV*	CP		1882	x	**M**	WC	*WC*	CS
1859	x	**M**	BK	*BK*	BT							

AJ41 (RBR)   RESTAURANT BUFFET

Mark 1. These vehicles were built as unclassified restaurant (RU). They were rebuilt with buffet counters and 23 fixed polypropylene chairs (RBS), then further refurbished by fitting fluorescent lighting and reclassified RBR. ETH 2X.

s Modified for use as servery vehicle with seating removed.

1953. Lot No. 30575 Swindon 1960. B4/B5 bogies. 36.5 t.
1961. Lot No. 30632 Swindon 1961. Commonwealth bogies. 39 t.

1953	s	**VN**	VS	*VS*	CP		1961	v	**G**	FM	*FM*	RL

AU51   CHARTER TRAIN STAFF COACHES

Mark 1. Converted from BCKs in 1988. Commonwealth bogies. ETH 2.

Lot No. 30732 Derby 1964. 37 t.

2833	(21270)	**BG**	E	*E*	OM
2834	(21267)	**GC**	E	*E*	OM

AT5G   HM THE QUEEN'S SALOON

Mark 3. Converted from a FO built 1972. Consists of a lounge, bedroom and bathroom for HM The Queen, and a combined bedroom and bathroom for the Queen's dresser. One entrance vestibule has double doors. Air conditioned. BT10 bogies. ETH 9X.

Lot No. 30886 Wolverton 1977. 36 t.

2903	(11001)	**RP**	NR	*RP*	ZN

AT5G HRH THE DUKE OF EDINBURGH'S SALOON

Mark 3. Converted from a TSO built 1972. Consists of a combined lounge/dining room, a bedroom and a shower room for the Duke, a kitchen and a valet's bedroom and bathroom. Air conditioned. BT10 bogies. ETH 15X.

Lot No. 30887 Wolverton 1977. 36 t.

2904	(12001)	**RP**	NR	*RP*	ZN

AT5G   ROYAL HOUSEHOLD SLEEPING CAR

Mark 3A. Built to similar specification as SLE 10646–732. 12 sleeping compartments for use of Royal Household with a fixed lower berth and a hinged upper berth. 2T plus shower room. Air conditioned. BT10 bogies. ETH 11X.

Lot No. 31002 Derby/Wolverton 1985. 44 t.

| 2915 | | **RP** | NR | *RP* | | ZN |

AT5G HRH THE PRINCE OF WALES'S DINING CAR

Mark 3. Converted from HST TRUK built 1976. Large kitchen retained, but dining area modified for Royal use seating up to 14 at central table(s). Air conditioned. BT10 bogies. ETH 13X.

Lot No. 31059 Wolverton 1988. 43 t.

| 2916 | (40512) | **RP** | NR | *RP* | | ZN |

AT5G   ROYAL KITCHEN/HOUSEHOLD DINING CAR

Mark 3. Converted from HST TRUK built 1977. Large kitchen retained and dining area slightly modified with seating for 22 Royal Household members. Air conditioned. BT10 bogies. ETH 13X.

Lot No. 31084 Wolverton 1990. 43 t.

| 2917 | (40514) | **RP** | NR | *RP* | | ZN |

AT5G   ROYAL HOUSEHOLD CARS

Mark 3. Converted from HST TRUKs built 1976/7. Air conditioned. BT10 bogies. ETH 10X.

Lot Nos. 31083 (31085*) Wolverton 1989. 41.05 t.

| 2918 | (40515) | | **RP** | NR | | ZN |
| 2919 | (40518) | * | **RP** | NR | | ZN |

AT5B   ROYAL HOUSEHOLD COUCHETTES

Mark 2B. Converted from BFK built 1969. Consists of luggage accommodation, guard's compartment, workshop area, 350 kW diesel generator and staff sleeping accommodation. B5 bogies. ETH2X.

Lot No. 31044 Wolverton 1986. 48 t.

| 2920 | (14109, 17109) | **RP** | NR | *RP* | | ZN |

Mark 2B. Converted from BFK built 1969. Consists of luggage accommodation, kitchen, brake control equipment and staff accommodation. B5 bogies. ETH7X.

Lot No. 31086 Wolverton 1990. 41.5 t.

| 2921 | (14107, 17107) | **RP** | NR | *RP* | | ZN |

AT5G HRH THE PRINCE OF WALES'S SLEEPING CAR

Mark 3B. BT10 bogies. Air conditioned. ETH 7X.

Lot No. 31035 Derby/Wolverton 1987.

| 2922 | | **RP** | NR | *RP* | | ZN |

▲ BR SR Green-liveried Mark 1 RBR 1696 at Blaenau Ffestiniog on 23/03/02.
Ivor Bufton

▼ BR SR Green-liveried Mark 1 FO 3114 at Blaenau Ffestiniog on 23/03/02.
Ivor Bufton

▲ GWR Chocolate & Cream-liveried Mark 1 TSO 4927 passes Gospel Oak on 19/02/05 during a "Buffer Puffer" Pathfinder railtour. **Robert Pritchard**

▼ BR Blue & Grey-liveried Mark 1 BCK 21246 is seen at Milton Keynes on 18/06/05. The coach is displaying a common problem with Mark 1 vehicles – peeling paint on the roof! **Mark Beal**

▲ BR Maroon-liveried Mark 1 BSK 35476 (99041) is used as a Locomotive Support Coach for steam loco 6233 "DUCHESS OF SUTHERLAND". Both are pictured here at Derby on 21/05/05. **Robert Pritchard**

▼ Riviera Trains Oxford blue & cream-liveried facelifted Mark 2A TSO 5322 at Gospel Oak on 19/02/05, next to the rear train loco 37406. **Robert Pritchard**

▲ BR Maroon-liveried Mark 2B TSO 5478, owned by West Coast Railway Company, at Bangor on 03/04/05. **Ivor Bufton**

▼ VSOE Northern Belle-liveried Mark 2D FO 3182 "WARWICK" at Chester on 10/09/03. **Ivor Bufton**

▲ First Great Western green-liveried Mark 2D BSO 9490 at Plymouth on 11/07/05, next to 57605 on the 23.50 Paddington–Penzance service. **Robert Pritchard**

▼ VSOE Northern Belle-liveried Mark 2D BFK 17167 at Worcester Shrub Hill on 10/07/04. **Stephen Widdowson**

▲ Six Arriva Trains-liveried Mark 2Fs found use on Rhymney line services in summer 2005. TSO 6035 is at Lisvane & Thornhill on 16/07/05. **Mark Beal**

▼ Anglia Railways-liveried Mark 2F DBSO 9704 at Ipswich on 21/06/05.
Rodney Lissenden

▲ Anglia Railways-liveried Mark 3A RFM 10241 at Ipswich on 12/07/05.
Robert Pritchard

▼ Virgin Trains-liveried Mark 3B FO 11067 at Ipswich on 12/07/05. One Anglia had several Virgin-liveried Mark 3 rakes in use during 2005 whilst their Mark 3 refurbishment programme was ongoing.
Robert Pritchard

▲ "One"-liveried Mark 3A TSO 12109 at Derby Litchurch Lane on 20/07/05 during a press launch following refurbishment for the Liverpool Street–Norwich route. This vehicle has a modified "high density" interior, with 80 seats almost all arranged unidirectionally. **Robert Pritchard**

▼ ScotRail Caledonian Sleepers-liveried Mark 3A SLEP 10508 at Fort William on 25/06/05. **Paul Robertson**

AT5G   ROYAL SALOON

Mark 3B. BT10 bogies. Air conditioned. ETH 6X.

Lot No. 31036 Derby/Wolverton 1987.

2923	**RP**	NR	*RP*	ZN

AD11 (FO)   OPEN FIRST

Mark 1. 42/– 2T. ETH 3. Many now fitted with table lamps.

3063–3069. Lot No. 30169 Doncaster 1955. B4 bogies. 33 t.
3096–3100. Lot No. 30576 BRCW 1959. B4 bogies. 33 t.

3064 and 3068 were numbered DB 975607 and DB 975606 for a time when in departmental service for British Railways.

3063	**BG**	VS		SL		3096	x **M**	BK	*BK*	BT
3064	**BG**	VS		SL		3097	**GC**	E	*E*	OM
3066	**RV**	RV	*RV*	CP		3098	x **CH**	RV	*RV*	CP
3068	**RV**	RV	*RV*	CP		3100	x **M**	E	*E*	OM
3069	**RV**	RV	*RV*	CP						

Later design with fluorescent lighting, aluminium window frames and Commonwealth bogies.

3105–3128. Lot No. 30697 Swindon 1962–63. 36 t.
3130–3150. Lot No. 30717 Swindon 1963. 36 t.

3128/36/41/3/4/6/7/8 were renumbered 1058/60/3/5/6/8/9/70 when reclassified RUO, then 3600/5/8/9/2/6/4/10 when declassified, but have since regained their original numbers. 3136 was numbered DB977970 for a time when in use with Serco Railtest as a Brake Force Runner.

3105	x **M**	WC	*WC*	CS		3128	x **M**	WC	*WC*	CS
3107	x **CH**	RV	*RV*	CP		3130	v **M**	WC	*WC*	CS
3110	x **M**	E	*E*	OM		3131	x **M**	E	*E*	OM
3112	x **CH**	RV	*RV*	CP		3132	x **M**	E	*E*	OM
3113	x **M**	WC	*WC*	CS		3133	x **M**	E	*E*	OM
3114	**G**	E	*E*	BN		3136	**M**	WC	*WC*	CS
3115	x **M**	BK		BT		3140	x **CH**	RV	*RV*	CP
3117	x **M**	WC	*WC*	CS		3141	**GC**	E	*E*	OM
3119	x **GC**	E	*E*	OM		3143	**M**	WC	*WC*	CS
3120	**GC**	E	*E*	OM		3144	x **M**	E	*E*	OM
3121	**GC**	E	*E*	OM		3146	**GC**	E	*E*	OM
3122	x **CH**	RV	*RV*	CP		3147	**GC**	E	*E*	OM
3123	**GC**	E	*E*	OM		3148	**BG**	RV	*RV*	CP
3124	**G**	E	*E*	OM		3149	**GC**	E	*E*	OM
3127	**G**	E	*E*	OM		3150	**G**	BK		BT

AD1D (FO)   OPEN FIRST

Mark 2D. Air conditioned. Stones equipment. 42/– 2T. B4 bogies. ETH 5.

† Interior modified to resemble a Pullman Car with new seating, tungsten lighting and table lights for VSOE "Northern Belle".

Lot No. 30821 Derby 1971–72. 34 t.

3174	†	**VN**	VS	*VS*	CP	3186			MA	DY
3181		**RV**	RV		CD	3188	**RV**	RV		CD
3182	†	**VN**	VS	*VS*	CP					

AD1E (FO)   OPEN FIRST

Mark 2E. Air conditioned. Stones equipment. 42/– 2T (41/– 2T 1W w, 36/– 2T p). B4 bogies. ETH 5.

r Refurbished with new seats.
u Fitted with power supply for Mk. 1 RBR.
† Interior modified to resemble a Pullman Car with new seating, tungsten lighting and table lights for VSOE "Northern Belle".

3255 was numbered 3525 for a time when fitted with a pantry.

Lot No. 30843 Derby 1972–73. 32.5 t. (35.8 t. †).

3223		**RV**	RV	*RV*	CP	3247	†	**VN**	VS	*VS*	CP
3228	du	**RV**	H	*RV*	CP	3255	dr	**FP**	H		OM
3229	d	**RV**	H	*RV*	CP	3261	dw	**FP**	H		CD
3231	p	**PC**	RA	*WT*	OM	3267	†	**VN**	VS	*VS*	CP
3232	dr	**FP**	H	*GW*	OO	3269	dr	**FP**	H		OM
3240		**RV**	RV	*RV*	CP	3273	†	**VN**	VS	*VS*	CP
3241	dr	**FP**	H	*GW*	OO	3275	†	**VN**	VS	*VS*	CP
3244	d	**RV**	H	*RV*	CP						

AD1F (FO)   OPEN FIRST

Mark 2F. Air conditioned. 3277–3318/58–81 have Stones equipment, others have Temperature Ltd. 42/– 2T. All now refurbished with power-operated vestibule doors, new panels and new seat trim. B4 bogies. d. ETH 5X.

3277–3318. Lot No. 30845 Derby 1973. 33.5 t.
3325–3428. Lot No. 30859 Derby 1973–74. 33.5 t.
3429–3438. Lot No. 30873 Derby 1974–75. 33.5 t.

r Further refurbished with table lamps, modified seats with burgundy seat trim and new m.a. sets.
s Further refurbished with table lamps and modified seats with burgundy seat trim.
u Fitted with power supply for Mk. 1 RBR.

3403 was numbered 6450 for a time when declassified.

3277		**AR**	H	*1A*	NC	3278	r	**V**	H		OY

3279	u	**AR**	H	*1A*	NC	3364	r	**V**	H	*RV*	CP
3285	s	**V**	H		OY	3366	s	**V**	H	*FM*	OY
3290		**AR**	H		CT	3368		**M**	H	*E*	OM
3292		**M**	H	*E*	OM	3369	s	**V**	H		CT
3295		**AR**	H	*1A*	NC	3373			H		BR
3299	r	**V**	H		KT	3374			H	*FM*	OY
3300	s	**V**	H		OM	3375		**AR**	H	*1A*	NC
3303		**AR**	H	*1A*	NC	3379	u	**AR**	H	*1A*	NC
3304	r	**V**	H	*RV*	CP	3381			H		Bramley
3309			H	*1A*	NC	3384	r	**V**	H	*RV*	CP
3312			H	*FM*	OY	3385	r	**V**	H	*FM*	OY
3313	r	**V**	H		KT	3386	r	**V**	H	*RV*	CP
3314	r	**V**	H	*RV*	CP	3387	s	**V**	H		MQ
3318		**M**	H	*E*	OM	3388		**AR**	H	*1A*	NC
3325	r	**V**	H	*RV*	CP	3389	s	**V**	H		CT
3326	r	**V**	H		KT	3390	r	**V**	H	*RV*	CP
3330	r	**V**	H	*RV*	CP	3392	r	**V**	H		KT
3331		**AR**	H	*1A*	NC	3395	r	**V**	H	*FM*	OY
3333	r	**V**	H	*RV*	CP	3397	r	**V**	H	*RV*	CP
3334		**AR**	H	*1A*	NC	3399	u	**AR**	H		NC
3336	u	**AR**	H	*1A*	NC	3400		**AR**	H		NC
3337	r	**V**	H		OM	3402	s	**V**	H		MQ
3338	u	**AR**	H	*1A*	NC	3403	s	**V**	H		CT
3340	r	**V**	H	*RV*	CP	3408	s	**V**	FM	*FM*	OY
3344	r	**V**	H	*RV*	CP	3411	s	**V**	H		MQ
3345	r	**V**	H	*RV*	CP	3414		**AR**	H	*1A*	NC
3348	r	**V**	H	*RV*	CP	3416			H	*1A*	NC
3350	r	**V**	H		KT	3417		**AR**	H	*1A*	NC
3351		**AR**	H	*1A*	NC	3424		**AR**	H	*1A*	NC
3352	r	**V**	H		KT	3425	s	**V**	H		MQ
3353	s	**V**	H		MQ	3426	r	**V**	H	*RV*	CP
3354	s	**V**	H		MQ	3428	s	**V**	H		CT
3356	r	**V**	H	*RV*	CP	3429	r	**V**	H		OM
3358		**AR**	H	*1A*	NC	3431	r	**V**	H		KT
3359	s	**V**	FM	*FM*	OY	3433	r	**V**	H		PY
3360	s		FM	*FM*	OY	3434	s	**V**	H		CT
3362	s		FM	*FM*	OY	3438	s	**V**	H		CT
3363	s	**V**	H		CT						

AG1E (FO (T))   OPEN FIRST (PANTRY)

Mark 2E. Air conditioned. Converted from FO. Fitted with pantry containing microwave oven and space for a trolley. 36/– 2T. B4 bogies. d. ETH 5X.

Lot No. 30843 Derby 1972–73. 32.5 t.

3520	(3253)	**FP**	H		BR	3523	(3238)	H	BR
3521	(3271)	**AR**	H		BR	3524	(3254)	H	BR
3522	(3236)	**FP**	H		BR				

AC21 (TSO)   OPEN STANDARD

Mark 1. These vehicles have 2+2 seating and are classified TSO ('Tourist second open'– a former LNER designation). –/64 2T. ETH 4.

3766. Lot No. 30079 York 1953. Commonwealth bogies (originally built with BR Mark 1 bogies). This coach has narrower seats than later vehicles. 36 t.

3766	x	**M**	WC	*WC*	CS	

AC21 (TSO)   OPEN STANDARD

Mark 1. These vehicles are a development of the above with fluorescent lighting and modified design of seat headrest. Built with BR Mark 1 bogies. –/64 2T. ETH 4.

4831–4836. Lot No. 30506 Wolverton 1959. Commonwealth bogies. 33 t.
4856. Lot No. 30525 Wolverton 1959–60. B4 bogies. 33 t.

4831	x	**M**	BK	*BK*	BT		4836	x	**M**	BK	*BK*	BT
4832	x	**M**	BK	*BK*	BT		4856	x	**M**	BK	*BK*	BT

Lot No. 30646 Wolverton 1961. Built with Commonwealth bogies, but BR Mark 1 bogies substituted by the SR. All now re-rebogied. 34 t B4, 36 t C.

4902	x B4	**CH**	RV	*RV*	CP		4912	x C	**M**	WC	*WC*	CS
4905	x C	**M**	WC	*WC*	CS							

Lot No. 30690 Wolverton 1961–62. Commonwealth bogies and aluminium window frames. 37 t.

4925		**G**	E	*E*	OM		4996	x	**M**	E	*E*	OM
4927	x	**CH**	RV	*RV*	CP		4998		**BG**	E	*E*	OM
4931	v	**M**	WC	*WC*	CS		4999		**BG**	E	*E*	OM
4940	x	**M**	WC	*WC*	CS		5002		**BG**	E	*E*	OM
4946	x	**M**	E	*E*	OM		5005		**BG**	E	*E*	OM
4949	x	**M**	E	*E*	OM		5007		**G**	E	*E*	OM
4951	x	**M**	WC	*WC*	CS		5008	x	**M**	E	*E*	OM
4954	v	**M**	WC	*WC*	CS		5009	x	**CH**	RV	*RV*	CP
4956		**BG**	E	*E*	OM		5023		**G**	E	*E*	OM
4958	v	**M**	WC	*WC*	CS		5027		**G**	E	*E*	OM
4959		**BG**	E	*E*	OM		5028	x	**M**	BK	*BK*	BT
4960	x	**M**	WC	*WC*	CS		5032	x	**M**	WC	*WC*	CS
4973	x	**M**	WC	*WC*	CS		5033	x	**M**	WC	*WC*	CS
4977		**G**	E		BN		5035	x	**M**	WC	*WC*	CS
4984	x	**M**	WC	*WC*	CS		5037		**G**	E	*E*	OM
4986		**G**	E	*E*	OM		5040	x	**CH**	RV	*RV*	CP
4991		**BG**	E	*E*	OM		5044	x	**M**	WC	*WC*	CS
4994	x	**M**	WC	*WC*	CS							

AC2Z (TSO)   OPEN STANDARD

Mark 2. Pressure ventilated. –/64 2T. B4 bogies. ETH 4.

Lot No. 30751 Derby 1965–67. 32 t.

5125	v **G**	FM	*FM*	RL	
5141	v **G**	FM		RL	
5148	v **RR**	H			TM
5157	v **CH**	H	*VT*	TM	
5171	v **G**	FM	*FM*	RL	
5177	v **CH**	H	*VT*	TM	
5179	v **RR**	H			TM
5183	v **RR**	H			TM
5186	v **RR**	H			TM
5191	v **CH**	H	*VT*	TM	
5193	v **LN**	H			TM
5194	v **RR**	H			TM
5198	v **CH**	H	*VT*	TM	
5199	v **G**	FM		RL	
5200	v **G**	FM	*FM*	RL	
5212	v **LN**	H			TM
5216	v **G**	FM	*FM*	RL	
5221	v **RR**	H			TM
5222	v **G**	FM	*FM*	RL	

AD2Z (SO)   OPEN STANDARD

Mark 2. Pressure ventilated. –/48 2T. B4 bogies. ETH 4.

Lot No. 30752 Derby 1966. 32 t.

5229	**PC**	WT	*WT*	OM	
5236	v **G**	FM	*FM*	RL	
5237	v **G**	FM	*FM*	RL	
5239	**PC**	WT	*WT*	OM	
5249	v **G**	FM	*FM*	RL	

AC2A (TSO)   OPEN STANDARD

Mark 2A. Pressure ventilated. –/64 2T (–/62 2T w). B4 bogies. ETH 4.

5276–5341. Lot No. 30776 Derby 1967–68. 32 t.
5350–5419. Lot No. 30787 Derby 1968. 32 t.

f Facelifted vehicles.

5276	f **RV**	RV	*RV*	CP	
5278	**PC**	WT	*WT*	OM	
5292	f **RV**	RV	*RV*	CP	
5299	**M**	WC	*WC*	CS	
5309	**CH**	RV	*RV*	CP	
5322	f **RV**	RV	*RV*	CP	
5331	**M**	E		TO	
5341	f **RV**	RV	*RV*	CP	
5350	**RV**	RV		CP	
5365	**RV**	RV	*RV*	CP	
5366	f **RV**	RV	*RV*	CP	
5376	**RV**	RV	*RV*	CP	
5386	w **M**	E		TO	
5412	w **M**	BK	*BK*	BT	
5419	w **PC**	WT	*WT*	OM	

AC2B (TSO)   OPEN STANDARD

Mark 2B. Pressure ventilated. –/62 2T. B4 bogies. ETH 4.

Note: 5482 was numbered DB977936 for a time when in departmental service
for British Railways.

Lot No. 30791 Derby 1969. 32 t.

5453	d **M**	WC	*WC*	CS	
5463	d **M**	WC	*WC*	CS	
5478	d **M**	WC	*WC*	CS	
5482	**M**	RP	*E*	OM	
5487	d **M**	WC	*WC*	CS	
5491	d **M**	WC	*WC*	CS	

AC2C (TSO)   OPEN STANDARD

Mark 2C. Pressure ventilated. –/62 2T. B4 bogies. ETH 4.

Lot No. 30795 Derby 1969–70. 32 t.

5569	d	**M**	WC	*WC*	CS		5600		**M**	WC		CS

AC2D (TSO)   OPEN STANDARD

Mark 2D. Air conditioned. Stones equipment. –/62 2T. B4 bogies. ETH 5.
r Refurbished with new seats and end luggage stacks. –/58 2T.

Lot No. 30822 Derby 1971. 33 t.

5631	dr	**FP**	H		OM		5700	dr	**FP**	H	*GW*	OO
5632	dr	**FP**	H		OM		5704		**M**	WC		CS
5636	dr	**FP**	H	*GW*	OO		5710	dr	**FP**	H	*GW*	OO
5647		**RV**	RV	*RV*	CP		5714		**M**	WC		CS
5657	dr	**FP**	H		OM		5727		**M**	WC		CS
5669	dr	**FP**	H	*GW*	OO		5737	dr	**FP**	H	*GW*	OO
5679	dr	**FP**	H	*GW*	OO		5740	dr	**FP**	H	*GW*	OO

AC2E (TSO)   OPEN STANDARD

Mark 2E. Air conditioned. Stones equipment. –/64 2T (w –/62 2T 1W). B4 bogies.
d (except 5756). ETH 5.

5744–5801. Lot No. 30837 Derby 1972. 33.5 t.
5810–5906. Lot No. 30844 Derby 1972–73. 33.5 t.

r Refurbished with new interior panelling.
s Refurbished with new interior panelling, modified design of seat headrest and centre luggage stack. –/60 2T (w –/58 2T 1W).
t Refurbished with new interior panelling and new seats.

5744		**FP**	H		BR		5788	r		H	*FM*	OY
5745	s	**V**	H		KT		5789	r pt		H	*FM*	OY
5746	r	**V**	H		KT		5791	wr		H	*RV*	CP
5748	r pt		H	*RV*	CP		5792	r		H	*RV*	CP
5750	s	**V**	H		KT		5793	wspt	**V**	H		KT
5752	wrpt		H	*RV*	CP		5794	wr		H	*RV*	CP
5754	ws	**V**	H		KT		5796	wr		H	*RV*	CP
5756		**M**	WC		CS		5797	r★		H	*FM*	BH
5769	r		H	*RV*	CP		5800		**AR**	H		CT
5773	s pt	**V**	H	*RV*	CP		5801	r	**V**	H		KT
5775	s	**V**	H		KT		5810	s	**V**	H		KT
5776	r		H	*RV*	CP		5812	wr		H	*FM*	OY
5778		**AR**	H	*1A*	NC		5814	r		H		OM
5779	r		H	*FM*	OY		5815	ws	**V**	H		KT
5780		**AR**	H		CT		5816	r pt		H		OM
5784	r	**V**	H		KT		5821	r pt	**V**	H		KT
5787	s	**V**	H		KT		5822	wspt	**V**	H		KT

5824	rw		H	*FM*	OY
5827	r		H	*FM*	OY
5828	ws	**V**	H		KT
5831		**AR**	H		CT
5836		**AR**	H		CT
5843	rw		H	*RV*	CP
5845	s	**V**	H		KT
5847	rw	**V**	H		KT
5852		**AR**	H		CT
5853	t	**M**	WC *WC*		CS
5859	s	**V**	H		KT
5863		**AR**	H	*1A*	NC
5866	r pt★		H	*FM*	BH
5868	s pt	**V**	H		KT
5869	t	**M**	WC *WC*		CS
5874	t	**M**	WC *WC*		CS
5876	s pt	**V**	H		KT
5881	ws	**V**	H		KT
5886	s	**V**	H		KT
5887	wr	**AR**	H	*1A*	NC
5888	wr		H	*FM*	OY
5889	s	**V**	H		KT
5893	s	**V**	H		KT
5897	r		H	*FM*	OY
5899	s	**V**	H		KT
5900	wspt	**V**	H		KT
5901	s	**V**	H		KT
5902	s	**V**	H		KT
5903	s	**V**	H		KT
5905	s	**V**	H	*RV*	CP
5906	wspt★		H	*FM*	BH

AC2F (TSO)   OPEN STANDARD

Mark 2F. Air conditioned. Temperature Ltd. equipment. Inter-City 70 seats. All were refurbished in the 1980s with power-operated vestibule doors, new panels and new seat trim. –/64 2T. (w –/62 2T 1W) B4 bogies. d. ETH 5X.

5908–5958. Lot No. 30846 Derby 1973. 33 t.
5959–6170. Lot No. 30860 Derby 1973–74. 33 t.
6171–6184. Lot No. 30874 Derby 1974–75. 33 t.

* Early Mark 2 style seats.

These vehicles have undergone a second refurbishment with carpets and new seat trim .
r Standard refurbished vehicles with new m.a. sets.

Former Cross-Country vehicles:

s Also fitted with centre luggage stack. –/60 2T.
t Also fitted with centre luggage stack and wheelchair space. –/58 2T 1W.

Former West Coast vehicles:

u As 'r' but with two wheelchair spaces. –/60 2T 2W.
† Standard refurbished vehicles with new seat trim.

5908	r	**V**	H		KT
5910	u	**V**	H	*AW*	CF
5911	s	**V**	RV *RV*		CP
5912	s	**V**	H	*FM*	OY
5913	s	**M**	WC *WC*		CS
5914	u	**V**	H		KT
5915	r	**V**	H		PY
5916	t		H		KT
5917	s	**V**	H		KT
5918	t	**V**	H		KT
5919	s pt	**V**	H	*FM*	OY
5920	†	**V**	H		MQ
5921		**AR**	H	*1A*	NC
5922		**AR**	H		CD
5924		**AR**	H		CD
5925	s pt★		H	*FM*	BH
5926			H	*1A*	NC
5927		**AR**	H		CT
5928		**AR**	H	*1A*	NC
5929		**AR**	H	*1A*	NC
5930	t	**V**	H		KT
5931	†w	**V**	H	*RV*	CP
5932	r	**V**	H	*RV*	CP
5933	r	**V**	H		KT

No.					
5934	r	**V**	H	*RV*	CP
5935		**AR**	H	*1A*	NC
5936		**AR**	H	*1A*	NC
5937	r	**V**	H	*RV*	CP
5939	r	**V**	H		PY
5940	u	**V**	H		KT
5941	r	**V**	H	*RV*	CP
5943	rw	**V**	H		KT
5944		**AR**	H	*1A*	NC
5945	r	**V**	H	*RV*	CP
5946	r	**V**	H	*RV*	CP
5947	s pt	**V**	H		KT
5948	u	**V**	H	*FM*	OY
5949	u	**V**	H		KT
5950		**AR**	H	*1A*	NC
5951	r	**V**	H		KT
5952	r	**V**	H	*RV*	CP
5954		**AR**	H	*1A*	NC
5955	r	**V**	H	*RV*	CP
5956			H		CT
5957	r	**V**	H		KT
5958	s★		H	*FM*	BH
5959	n	**AR**	H	*1A*	NC
5960	s	**V**	H	*FM*	OY
5961	s pt	**V**	RV	*RV*	CP
5962	s pt	**V**	H		KT
5963	r	**V**	H	*RV*	CP
5964		**AR**	H	*1A*	NC
5965	t	**M**	WC	*WC*	CS
5966		**AR**	H	*1A*	NC
5967	t	**V**	H		KT
5968		**AR**	H	*1A*	NC
5969	u	**V**	H	*RV*	CP
5971	s	**V**	RV	*AW*	CF
5973		**AR**	H		CT
5975	s	**V**	H		KT
5976	t	**V**	RV	*AW*	CF
5977	r	**V**	H		KT
5978	r	**V**	H		KT
5980	r	**V**	H		KT
5981	s★		H	*FM*	BH
5983	s	**V**	H	*FM*	OY
5984	r	**V**	H	*RV*	CP
5985		**AR**	H	*1A*	NC
5986	r	**V**	H	*RV*	CP
5987	r	**V**	H	*RV*	CP
5988	r	**V**	H		KT
5989	t	**V**	H	*FM*	OY
5991	s	**V**	H	*FM*	OY
5993	*	**AR**	H	*1A*	NC
5994	r	**V**	H		KT
5995	s	**V**	H	*FM*	OY
5996	s pt	**V**	H		KT
5997	r	**V**	H	*RV*	CP
5998		**AR**	H	*1A*	NC
5999	s	**V**	H		KT
6000	t	**V**	H		KT
6001	u	**V**	H	*FM*	OY
6002	†	**V**	H		MQ
6005	r	**V**	H		KT
6006		**AR**	H	*1A*	NC
6008	s	**V**	RV	*AW*	CF
6009	r	**V**	H		KT
6010	s	**V**	H		KT
6011	s	**V**	H		KT
6012	r	**V**	H		KT
6013	s	**M**	WC	*WC*	CS
6014	s pt		H		KT
6015	t	**V**	H		KT
6016	r	**V**	H		KT
6018	t	**V**	H		KT
6021	r	**V**	H		KT
6022	s	**V**	H		KT
6024	s	**V**	H		OM
6025	t	**V**	H		KT
6026	s	**V**	H		KT
6027	u	**V**	H	*AW*	CF
6028		**AR**	H	*1A*	NC
6029	r	**V**	H		KT
6030	t	**V**	H		KT
6031	r	**V**	H		KT
6034		**AR**	H	*1A*	NC
6035	t★	**AV**	E	*AW*	CF
6036	*	**M**		*E*	OM
6037		**AR**	H		OM
6038	s	**V**	H		OM
6041	s	**V**	H		KT
6042		**AR**	H	*1A*	NC
6043	†	**V**	H	*RV*	CP
6045	†w	**V**	H	*FM*	OY
6046	s	**V**	H	*FM*	OY
6047	†n*	**V**	H		CT
6049	r	**V**	H	*FM*	OY
6050	s		H		KT
6051	r	**V**	H	*RV*	CP
6052	tw		H		KT
6053	*	**AR**	H	*1A*	NC
6054	r	**V**	H	*RV*	CP
6055	†	**V**	H		KT
6056	†	**V**	H	*RV*	CP
6059	s	**V**	H	*FM*	OY
6061	s pt	**V**	H		KT

6062	†	**V**	H		KT
6063	†w	**V**	H		CT
6064	s	**V**	RV	*AW*	CF
6065	r	**V**	H		KT
6066	s★	**AV**	E	*AW*	CF
6067	s pt	**V**	RV	*RV*	CP
6073	s	**V**	H		KT
6100	†*	**V**	H		CT
6101	r	**V**	H	*RV*	CP
6103		**AR**	H	*1A*	NC
6104	r	**V**	H	*RV*	CP
6105	tpt	**V**	H		KT
6107	r	**V**	H	*AW*	CF
6110			H		CD
6111	†	**V**	H	*RV*	CP
6112	s pt	**V**	H		KT
6113	†	**V**	H	*RV*	CP
6115	s		H		KT
6116	†	**V**	H		KT
6117	t★	**WX**	H	*WX*	PM
6119	s	**V**	RV	*AW*	CF
6120	s	**V**	H		KT
6121	†	**V**	H	*FM*	OY
6122	s★	**WX**	H	*WX*	PM
6123		**AR**	H	*1A*	NC
6124	s pt★	**AV**	E		TO
6134	†	**V**	H	*FM*	OY
6135	s		H		KT
6136	r	**V**	H		KT
6137	s pt	**V**	RV	*AW*	CF
6138	†	**V**	H	*RV*	CP
6139	n*	**M**	H	*E*	OM
6141	u	**V**	H	*RV*	CP
6142	†*	**V**	H	*RV*	CP
6144	†*	**V**	H		CT
6145	s pt	**V**	H		KT
6146	*	**AR**	H	*1A*	NC
6148	s		H		KT
6149	u	**V**	H		PY
6150	s		H		KT
6151	†*	**V**	H	*FM*	OY
6152	*	**M**	H	*E*	OM
6153	†	**V**	H		KT
6154	r pt		H		KT
6155	*	**AR**	H		CT
6157	s	**V**	H	*RV*	CP
6158	r	**V**	H	*RV*	CP
6159	s pt	**V**	H		KT
6160	*	**AR**	H	*1A*	NC
6161	†*	**V**	H		CT
6162	s pt	**V**	RV	*AW*	CF
6163	r	**V**	RV	*RV*	CP
6164	†	**V**	H	*FM*	OY
6165	r	**V**	H		KT
6166			H	*1A*	NC
6167		**AR**	H	*1A*	NC
6168	s★		H	*FM*	BH
6170	s★	**AV**	E	*AW*	CF
6171	†	**V**	H	*RV*	CP
6172	s	**V**	H		KT
6173	s★	**WX**	H	*WX*	PM
6174		**AR**	H	*1A*	NC
6175	r	**V**	H		KT
6176	t	**V**	H		OM
6177	s	**V**	RV	*RV*	CP
6179	r	**V**	H		KT
6180	†w	**V**	H	*RV*	CP
6181	†wn	**V**	H		MQ
6182	s	**V**	H		KT
6183	s	**V**	RV	*AW*	CF
6184	s	**V**	H		KT

AC2D (TSO)   OPEN STANDARD

Mark 2D. Air conditioned (Stones). Rebuilt from FO with new style 2+2 seats. – /58 2T. (–/58 1T*). B4 bogies. d. ETH 5X.

Lot No. 30821 Derby 1971–72. 33.5 t.

* One toilet converted to store room.

6200	(3198)	**FP**	H		BR			
6202	(3191)*	**FP**	H		KT			
6203	(3180)	**FP**	H		BR			
6206	(3183)	**FP**	H		BR			
6207	(3204)	**FP**	H		BR			
6212	(3176)	**FP**	H		BR			
6213	(3208)	**FP**	H		BR			
6219	(3213)	**FP**	H		BR			
6221	(3173)	**FP**	H		BR			
6226	(3203)	**FP**	H		BR			

AX51   GENERATOR VAN

Mark 1. Converted from NEA/NHA in 2003 to generator vans for use on the Southern Region power upgrade project. B5 bogies.

6260. Lot No. 30400 Pressed Steel 1957–58.
6261. Lot No. 30323 Pressed Steel 1957.
6262. Lot No. 30228 Metro-Cammell 1957–58.
6263. Lot No. 30163 Pressed Steel 1957.
6264. Lot No. 30173 York 1956.

6260	(81450, 92116)	**NR**	NR	*E*	LU
6261	(81284, 92988)	**NR**	NR	*E*	LU
6262	(81064, 92928)	**Y**	NR	*E*	LU
6263✓	(81231, 92961)	**Y**	NR	*E*	DY
6264	(80971, 92923)	**Y**	NR	*E*	DY

AX51   BRAKE GENERATOR VAN

Mark 1. Renumbered 1989 from BR departmental series. Converted from NDA in 1973 to three-phase supply brake generator van for use with HST trailers. Modified 1999 for use with loco-hauled stock. B5 bogies.

Lot No. 30400 Pressed Steel 1958.

6310	(81448, 975325)	**CH**	RV	*RV*	CP

AX51   GENERATOR VAN

Mark 1. Converted from NDA in 1992 to generator vans for use on Anglo-Scottish sleeping car services. Now normally used on trains hauled by steam locomotives. B4 bogies. ETH75.

6311. Lot No. 30162 Pressed Steel 1958. 37.25 t.
6312. Lot No. 30224 Cravens 1956. 37.25 t.
6313. Lot No. 30484 Pressed Steel 1958. 37.25 t.

6311	(80903, 92911)	**B**	E	*E*	OM
6312	(81023, 92925)	**PC**	WC	*WC*	CS
6313	(81553, 92167)	**E**	P	*VS*	SL

NW51   DESIRO EMU BARRIER VEHICLE

Mark 1. Converted from GUVs with bodies removed and B4 bogies for use as Eurostar barrier vehicles but modified in 2003 by LNWR Co., Crewe for current use.

6321. Lot No. 30343 York 1957. 40 t.
6322/23. Lot No. 30616 Pressed Steel 1959–60. 40 t.
6324. Lot No. 30403 Glasgow 1958–60. 40 t.
6325. Lot No. 30417 Pressed Steel 1958–59. 40 t.

6321	(86515, 96385)	**B**	SM	*FL*	CP

6322	(86859, 96386)	**B**	SM	*FL*	CP
6323	(86973, 96387)	**B**	SM	*FL*	CP
6324	(86562, 96388)	**B**	SM	*FL*	CP
6325	(86135, 96389)	**B**	SM	*FL*	CP

GS5 (HSBV)   HST BARRIER VEHICLE

Renumbered from BR departmental series, or converted from various types.
B4 bogies (Commonwealth bogies *).

6330. Mark 2A. Lot No. 30786 Derby 1968. 32 t.
6336/38/44. Mark 1. Lot No. 30715 Gloucester 1962. 31 t.
6340. Mark 1. Lot No. 30669 Swindon 1962. 36 t.
6346. Mark 2A. Lot No. 30777 Derby 1967. 31.5 t.
6348. Mark 1. Lot No. 30163 Pressed Steel 1957. 31.5 t.

6330	(14084, 975629)		**G**	A	*GW*	LA
6336	(81591, 92185)		**G**	A	*GW*	LA
6338	(81581, 92180)		**G**	A	*GW*	LA
6340	(21251, 975678)	*	**G**	A	*GW*	LA
6344	(81263, 92080)		**GN**	A	*GN*	EC
6346	(9422)		**GN**	A	*GN*	EC
6348	(81233, 92963)		**G**	A	*GW*	LA

AV5A/AV5C (MFBV)   MARK 4 BARRIER VEHICLE

Mark 2A/2C. Converted from FK* or BSO. B4 bogies.

6352/3. Mark 2A. Lot No. 30774 Derby 1968. 33 t.
6354/5. Mark 2C. Lot No. 30820 Derby 1970. 32 t.
6358/9. Mark 2A. Lot No. 30788 Derby 1968. 31.5 t.

6352	(13465, 19465)	*	**GN**	H	*GN*	BN
6353	(13478, 19478)	*	**GN**	H	*GN*	BN
6354	(9459)		**GN**	H	*GN*	BN
6355	(9477)		**GN**	H	*GN*	BN
6358	(9432)		**GN**	H	*GN*	BN
6359	(9429)		**GN**	H	*GN*	BN

AW51   EMU TRANSLATOR VEHICLE

Mark 1. Converted 1992 from BG. BR Mark 1 bogies.

6364. Mark 1. Lot No. 30039 Derby 1954. 32 t.
6365. Mark 1. Lot No. 30323 Pressed Steel 1957. 32 t.

6364	(80565)	**RR**	MA	*CT*	SI
6365	(81296, 84296)	**RR**	MA	*CT*	SI

AW51   EMU TRANSLATOR VEHICLE

Mark 1. Converted 1980 from RUO. Commonwealth bogies.

Lot No. 30647 Wolverton 1959–61. 36 t.

6376	(1021, 975973)	**P**	P	*FL*	ZJ
6377	(1042, 975975)	**P**	P	*FL*	ZJ
6378	(1054, 975971)	**P**	P	*FL*	ZJ
6379	(1059, 975972)	**P**	P	*FL*	ZJ

GS51 (HSBV)   HST BARRIER VEHICLE

Mark 1. Converted from BG in 1994–5. B4 bogies.

6392. Lot No. 30715 Gloucester 1962. 29.5 t.
6393/96/97. Lot No. 30716 Gloucester 1962. 29.5 t.
6394. Lot No. 30162 Pressed Steel 1956–57. 30.5 t.
6395. Lot No. 30484 Pressed Steel 1958. 30.5 t.
6398/99. Lot No. 30400 Pressed Steel 1957–58. 30.5 t.

6392	(81588, 92183)	**P**	P	*MM*	NL
6393	(81609, 92196)	**P**	P	*MM*	NL
6394	(80878, 92906)	**P**	P	*MM*	NL
6395	(81506, 92148)	**P**	MA	*MM*	NL
6396	(81607, 92195)	**P**	P	*MM*	NL
6397	(81600, 92190)	**P**	P	*MM*	NL
6398	(81471, 92126)	**MA**	MA	*MM*	NL
6399	(81367, 92994)	**MA**	MA	*MM*	NL

AG2C (TSOT)   OPEN STANDARD (TROLLEY)

Mark 2C. Converted from TSO by removal of one seating bay and replacing this by a counter with a space for a trolley. Adjacent toilet removed and converted to steward's washing area/store. Pressure ventilated. –/55 1T. B4 bogies. ETH 4.

Lot No. 30795 Derby 1969–70. 32.5 t.

6528	(5592)	**M**	WC	*WC*	CS

AN1F (RLO)   SLEEPER RECEPTION CAR

Mark 2F. Converted from FO, these vehicles consist of pantry, microwave cooking facilities, seating area for passengers, telephone booth and staff toilet. 6703–8 also have a bar. Converted at RTC, Derby (6700), Ilford (6701–5) and Derby (6706–8). Air conditioned. 6700/1/3/5/–8 have Stones equipment and 6702/4 have Temperature Ltd. equipment. 26/– 1T. B4 bogies. d. ETH 5X.

Advertising Livery: 6703 is "Visit Scotland" – silver with broad blue tartan stripe down one end.

6700–2/4/8. Lot No. 30859 Derby 1973–74. 33.5 t.
6703/5–7. Lot No. 30845 Derby 1973. 33.5 t.

6700	(3347)	**CS**	H	*SR*	IS
6701	(3346)	**CS**	H	*SR*	IS
6702	(3421)	**CS**	H	*SR*	IS
6703	(3308)	**AL**	H	*SR*	IS
6704	(3341)	**CS**	H	*SR*	IS
6705	(3310, 6430)	**CS**	H	*SR*	IS

6706	(3283, 6421)	**CS**	H	*SR*	IS
6707	(3276, 6418)	**CS**	H	*SR*	IS
6708	(3370)	**CS**	H	*SR*	IS

AN1D (RMBF)　　　　MINIATURE BUFFET CAR

Mark 2D. Converted from TSOT by the removal of another seating bay and fitting a proper buffet counter with boiler and microwave oven. Now converted to first class with new seating and end luggage stacks. Air conditioned. Stones equipment. 30/– 1T. B4 bogies. d. ETH 5.

Lot No. 30822 Derby 1971. 33 t.

6720	(5622, 6652)	**FP**	H		OM
6721	(5627, 6660)	**FP**	H	*GW*	OO
6722	(5736, 6661)	**FP**	H	*GW*	OO
6723	(5641, 6662)	**FP**	H	*GW*	OO
6724	(5721, 6665)	**FP**	H	*GW*	OO

AC2F (TSO)　　　　　OPEN STANDARD

Mark 2F. Renumbered from FO and declassified in 1985–6. Converted 1990 to TSO with mainly unidirectional seating and power-operated sliding doors. Air conditioned. 6800–14 were converted by BREL Derby and have Temperature Ltd. air conditioning. 6815–29 were converted by RFS Industries Doncaster and have Stones air conditioning. –/74 2T. B4 bogies. d. ETH 5X.

6800–07. 6810–12. 6813–14. 6819/22/28. Lot No. 30859 Derby 1973–74. 33 t.
6808–6809. Lot No. 30873 Derby 1974–75. 33.5 t.
6815–18. 6820–21. 6823–27. 6829. Lot No. 30845 Derby 1973. 33 t.

6800	(3323, 6435)	**AR**	H		CT
6801	(3349, 6442)	**AR**	H	*1A*	NC
6802	(3339, 6439)	**AR**	H	*1A*	NC
6803	(3355, 6443)	**AR**	H	*1A*	NC
6804	(3396, 6449)		H		CT
6805	(3324, 6436)	**AR**	H	*1A*	NC
6806	(3342, 6440)	**AR**	H	*1A*	NC
6807	(3423, 6452)		H		CT
6808	(3430, 6454)	**AR**	H	*1A*	NC
6809	(3435, 6455)	**AR**	H		CT
6810	(3404, 6451)	**AR**	H	*1A*	NC
6811	(3327, 6437)	**AR**	H	*1A*	NC
6812	(3394, 6448)	**AR**	H	*1A*	NC
6813	(3410, 6463)		H		CT
6814	(3422, 6465)	**AR**	H	*1A*	NC
6815	(3282, 6420)	**AR**	H	*1A*	NC
6816	(3316, 6461)	**AR**	H		CT
6817	(3311, 6431)	**AR**	H	*1A*	NC
6818	(3298, 6427)	**AR**	H	*1A*	NC
6819	(3365, 6446)	**AR**	H	*1A*	NC
6820	(3320, 6434)	**AR**	H	*1A*	NC
6821	(3281, 6458)	**AR**	H	*1A*	NC

6822	(3376, 6447)	**AR**	H	*1A*	NC
6823	(3289, 6424)	**AR**	H	*1A*	NC
6824	(3307, 6429)	**AR**	H	*1A*	NC
6825	(3301, 6460)	**AR**	H		CT
6826	(3294, 6425)	**AR**	H	*1A*	NC
6827	(3306, 6428)	**AR**	H		CT
6828	(3380, 6464)	**AR**	H	*1A*	NC
6829	(3288, 6423)	**AR**	H	*1A*	NC

AH2Z (BSOT) OPEN BRAKE STANDARD (MICRO-BUFFET)

Mark 2. Converted from BSO by removal of one seating bay and replacing this by a counter with a space for a trolley. Adjacent toilet removed and converted to a steward's washing area/store. –/23 0T. B4 bogies. ETH 4.

Lot No. 30757 Derby 1966. 31 t.

| 9101 | (9398) | v | **CH** | H | *VT* | TM |
| 9104 | (9401) | v | **G** | FM | *FM* | RL |

AE2Z (BSO)   OPEN BRAKE STANDARD

Mark 2. These vehicles use the same body shell as the Mark 2 BFK and have first class seat spacing and wider tables. Pressure ventilated. –/31 1T. B4 bogies. ETH 4.

Lot No. 30757 Derby 1966. 31.5 t.

| 9391 | | **PC** | WT | *WT* | OM | | 9392 | v | **G** | FM | *FM* | RL |

AE2A (BSO)   OPEN BRAKE STANDARD

Mark 2A. These vehicles use the same body shell as the Mark 2A BFK and have first class seat spacing and wider tables. Pressure ventilated. –/31 1T. B4 bogies. ETH 4.

9419. Lot No. 30777 Derby 1970. 31.5 t.
9428. Lot No. 30820 Derby 1970. 31.5 t.

| 9419 | | **DR** | DR | *DR* | KM | | 9428 | | **DR** | DR | *DR* | KM |

AE2C (BSO)   OPEN BRAKE STANDARD

Mark 2C. Pressure ventilated. –/31 1T. B4 bogies. ETH 4.

Lot No. 30798 Derby 1970. 32 t.

| 9440 | d | **M** | WC | *WC* | CS | | 9448 | d | **M** | WC | *WC* | CS |

AE2D (BSO)   OPEN BRAKE STANDARD

Mark 2D. Air conditioned (Stones). –/31 1T. B4 bogies. d. pg. ETH 5.

r Refurbished with new interior panelling.
s Refurbished with new seating –/22 1TD.

w Facelifted –/28 1W 1T.

Lot No. 30824 Derby 1971. 33 t.

9479	r		H	FM	OY		9490	s	FP	H	GW	OO
9480		FP	H		KT		9492	w	FP	H		OM
9481	s	FP	H	GW	OO		9493	s	FP	H	GW	OO
9488	s	FP	H	GW	OO		9494	s	FP	H		OM
9489	r	V	H		KT							

AE2E (BSO)   OPEN BRAKE STANDARD

Mark 2E. Air conditioned (Stones). –/32 1T. B4 bogies. d. pg. ETH 5.

Lot No. 30838 Derby 1972. 33 t.

r Refurbished with new interior panelling.
s Refurbished with modified design of seat headrest and new interior panelling.
w Facelifted –/28 1W 1T.

9496	r★		H	FM	OY		9504	s	V	H	RV	CP
9497	r★		H	FM	BH		9505	s★		H	FM	BH
9498	r	V	H		KT		9506	s★	WX	H	WX	PM
9500	r		H	FM	OY		9507	s	V	H	AW	CF
9501	w	FP	H		OM		9508	s	V	H		KT
9502	s	V	H		KT		9509	s	V	H	RV	CP
9503	s	V	H	RV	CP							

AE2F (BSO)   OPEN BRAKE STANDARD

Mark 2F. Air conditioned (Temperature Ltd.). All now refurbished with power-operated vestibule doors, new panels and seat trim. All now further refurbished with carpets and new m.a. sets. –/32 1T. B4 bogies. d. pg. ETH5X.

Lot No. 30861 Derby 1974. 34 t.

9513		V	H	FM	OY		9526	n★		H	RV	CP
9516	n	V	H	FM	OY		9527	n	V		RV	AW	CF
9520	n	V	RV	AW	CF		9529	n	V		RV	RV	CP
9521	★	AV	E	AW	CF		9531		V		RV	RV	CP
9522		V	H	FM	OY		9537	n	V		H	RV	CP
9523		V	H		KT		9538		V	H		KT
9524	n★	AV	E		TO		9539		M	WC	WC	CS
9525		WX	H	WX	PM							

AF2F (DBSO) DRIVING OPEN BRAKE STANDARD

Mark 2F. Air conditioned (Temperature Ltd.). Push & pull (t.d.m. system). Converted from BSO, these vehicles originally had half cabs at the brake end. They have since been refurbished and have had their cabs widened and the cab-end gangways removed. –/30 1W 1T. B4 bogies. d. pg. Cowcatchers. ETH 5X.

9701–9710. Lot No. 30861 Derby 1974. Converted Glasgow 1979. Disc brakes. 34 t.

9711–9713. Lot No. 30861 Derby 1974. Converted Glasgow 1985. 34 t.
9714. Lot No. 30861 Derby 1974. Converted Glasgow 1986. Disc brakes. 34 t.

9701	(9528)	**AR**	H	1A	NC	9709	(9515)	**AR**	H 1A	NC
9702	(9510)	**AR**	H	1A	NC	9710	(9518)	1	H 1A	NC
9703	(9517)	**AR**	H	1A	NC	9711	(9532)	**AR**	H 1A	NC
9704	(9512)	**AR**	H	1A	NC	9712	(9534)	**AR**	H 1A	NC
9705	(9519)	**AR**	H	1A	NC	9713	(9535)	**AR**	H 1A	NC
9707	(9511)	**AR**	H	1A	NC	9714	(9536)	**AR**	H 1A	NC
9708	(9530)	**AR**	H	1A	NC					

AE4E (BUO)   UNCLASSIFIED OPEN BRAKE

Mark 2E. Converted from TSO with new seating for use on Anglo-Scottish overnight services by Railcare, Wolverton. Air conditioned. Stones equipment. B4 bogies. d. –/31 2T. B4 bogies. ETH 4X.

9801–9803. Lot No. 30837 Derby 1972. 33.5 t.
9804–9810. Lot No. 30844 Derby 1972–73. 33.5 t.

9800	(5751)	**CS**	H	SR	IS	9806	(5840)	**CS**	H SR	IS
9801	(5760)	**CS**	H	SR	IS	9807	(5851)	**CS**	H SR	IS
9802	(5772)	**CS**	H	SR	IS	9808	(5871)	**CS**	H SR	IS
9803	(5799)	**CS**	H	SR	IS	9809	(5890)	**CS**	H SR	IS
9804	(5826)	**CS**	H	SR	IS	9810	(5892)	**CS**	H SR	IS
9805	(5833)	**CS**	H	SR	IS					

AJ1G (RFM)   RESTAURANT BUFFET FIRST (MODULAR)

Mark 3A. Air conditioned. Converted from HST TRFKs, RFBs and FOs. Refurbished with table lamps and burgundy seat trim (except *). 18/– plus two seats for staff use (*24/–). BT10 bogies. d. ETH 14X.

10200–10211. Lot No. 30884 Derby 1977. 39.8 t.
10212–10229. Lot No. 30878 Derby 1975–76. 39.8 t.
10230–10260. Lot No. 30890 Derby 1979. 39.8 t.

Non-standard Livery: 10211 is EWS dark maroon.

10200	(40519)	*		P	1A	NC	10215	(11032)	**V**	P	WI
10201	(40520)	**V**		P		LT	10216	(11041)	* **AR**	P 1A	NC
10202	(40504)	**V**		P	E	WB	10217	(11051)	**V**	P E	OM
10203	(40506)	* **AR**	P	1A		NC	10218	(11053)	**V**	P	LT
10204	(40502)	**V**		P		WI	10219	(11047)	**V**	P E	OM
10205	(40503)	**V**		P		LT	10220	(11050)	**V**	P	CT
10206	(40507)	**V**		P	1A	NC	10221	(11012)	**V**	P	CT
10207	(40516)	**V**		P		CT	10223	(11043)	* **AR**	P 1A	NC
10208	(40517)	**V**		P		WI	10224	(11062)	**V**	P	LT
10209	(40508)	**V**		P		CT	10225	(11014)	**V**	P	LT
10210	(40509)	**V**		P		CT	10226	(11015)	**V**	P	WI
10211	(40510)	**0**		E	E	TO	10227	(11057)	**V**	P	CT
10212	(11049)	**V**		P	E	WB	10228	(11035)	* **AR**	P 1A	NC
10213	(11050)	**V**		P		LT	10229	(11059)	**1**	P	ZB
10214	(11034)	* **AR**	P	1A		NC	10230	(10021)	**1**	P	LT

10231	(10016)	**V**	P	*CD*	OY	10247	(10011)	* **AR**	P	*1A*	NC
10232	(10027)	**V**	P		LT	10248	(10005)	**V**	P		CT
10233	(10013)	**V**	P		LT	10249	(10012)	**V**	P		WI
10234	(10004)	**V**	P		CT	10250	(10020)	**V**	P		LT
10235	(10015)	**V**	P	*CD*	OY	10251	(10024)	**V**	P		CT
10236	(10018)	**V**	P		WI	10252	(10008)	**V**	P		CT
10237	(10022)	**V**	P		PC	10253	(10026)	**V**	P		LT
10238	(10017)	**V**	P		CT	10254	(10006)	**V**	P		CT
10240	(10003)	**V**	P		LT	10255	(10010)	**V**	P		WI
10241	(10009)	* **AR**	P	*1A*	NC	10256	(10028)	**V**	P		LT
10242	(10002)	**V**	P		WI	10257	(10007)	**V**	P	*E*	OM
10245	(10019)	**V**	P		WI	10259	(10025)	**V**	P		LT
10246	(10014)	**V**	P		PC	10260	(10001)	**V**	P		LT

AJ1J/AG2J (RFM/RSB)   RESTAURANT BUFFET

Mark 4. Air conditioned. BT41 bogies. ETH 6X. All except vehicles marked *
now rebuilt with standard class seating with bar adjacent to seating area instead
of adjacent to end of coach and known as "Mallard" stock. –/30 1T (20/– 1T*).

Lot No. 31045 Metro-Cammell 1989 onwards. 43.2 t (45.5 t*).

10300		**GN**	H	*GN*	BN	10317	**GN**	H *GN* BN
10301		**GN**	H	*GN*	BN	10318	**GN**	H *GN* BN
10302	*	**GN**	H	*GN*	BN	10319	**GN**	H *GN* BN
10303		**GN**	H	*GN*	BN	10320	**GN**	H *GN* BN
10304		**GN**	H	*GN*	BN	10321	**GN**	H *GN* BN
10305		**GN**	H	*GN*	BN	10323	**GN**	H *GN* BN
10306		**GN**	H	*GN*	BN	10324	**GN**	H *GN* BN
10307		**GN**	H	*GN*	BN	10325	**GN**	H *GN* BN
10308		**GN**	H	*GN*	BN	10326	**GN**	H *GN* BN
10309		**GN**	H	*GN*	BN	10328	**GN**	H *GN* BN
10310		**GN**	H	*GN*	BN	10329	**GN**	H *GN* BN
10311		**GN**	H	*GN*	BN	10330	**GN**	H *GN* BN
10312		**GN**	H	*GN*	BN	10331	**GN**	H *GN* BN
10313		**GN**	H	*GN*	BN	10332	**GN**	H *GN* BN
10315		**GN**	H	*GN*	BN	10333	**GN**	H *GN* BN

AU4G (SLEP)   SLEEPING CAR WITH PANTRY

Mark 3A. Air conditioned. Retention toilets. 12 compartments with a fixed lower
berth and a hinged upper berth, plus an attendants compartment. 2T BT10
bogies. ETH 7X.

Non-standard Livery: 10546 is EWS dark maroon.

Lot No. 30960 Derby 1981–83. 41 t.

10501	d	**CS**	P	*SR*	IS	10507	d	**CS**	P	*SR*	IS
10502	d	**CS**	P	*SR*	IS	10508	d	**CS**	P	*SR*	IS
10504	d	**CS**	P	*SR*	IS	10510	d		P		ZH
10506	d	**CS**	P	*SR*	IS	10513	d	**CS**	P	*SR*	IS

10515	d		P		IS
10516	d	**CP**	P	*SR*	IS
10519	d	**CS**	P	*SR*	IS
10520	d	**CS**	P	*SR*	IS
10522	d	**CS**	P	*SR*	IS
10523	d	**CP**	P	*SR*	IS
10526	d	**CS**	P	*SR*	IS
10527	d	**CS**	P	*SR*	IS
10529	d	**CS**	P	*SR*	IS
10531	d	**CS**	P	*SR*	IS
10532	d	**FP**	P	*GW*	PZ
10534	d	**FP**	P	*GW*	PZ
10538	d		P		KT
10539	d		P		KT
10542	d	**CS**	P	*SR*	IS
10543	d	**CS**	P	*SR*	IS
10544	d	**CS**	P	*SR*	IS
10546	d	**O**	E	*E*	TO
10547	d		P		IS
10548	d	**CP**	P	*SR*	IS
10551	d	**CS**	P	*SR*	IS
10553	d	**CS**	P	*SR*	IS
10555	d		P		KT
10559	d		P		KT
10561	d	**CS**	P	*SR*	IS
10562	d	**CP**	P	*SR*	IS
10563	d	**FP**	P	*GW*	PZ
10565	d	**CS**	P	*SR*	IS
10569	d	**PC**	VS		CP
10580	d	**CS**	P	*SR*	IS
10584	d	**FP**	P	*GW*	PZ
10588	d	**FP**	P	*GW*	PZ
10589	d	**FP**	P	*GW*	PZ
10590	d	**FP**	P	*GW*	PZ
10594	d	**FP**	P	*GW*	PZ
10596	d		P		KT
10597	d	**CS**	P	*SR*	IS
10598	d	**CS**	P	*SR*	IS
10600	d	**CP**	P	*SR*	IS
10601	d	**FP**	P	*GW*	PZ
10605	d	**CS**	P	*SR*	IS
10607	d	**CS**	P	*SR*	IS
10610	d	**CS**	P	*SR*	IS
10612	d	**FP**	P	*GW*	PZ
10613	d	**CS**	P	*SR*	IS
10614	d	**CS**	P	*SR*	IS
10616	d	**FP**	P	*GW*	PZ
10617	d	**CS**	P	*SR*	IS

AS4G/AQ4G* (SLE/SLED*)   SLEEPING CAR

Mark 3A. Air conditioned. Retention toilets. 13 compartments with a fixed lower berth and a hinged upper berth (* 11 compartments with a fixed lower berth and a hinged upper berth + one compartment for a disabled person). 2T. BT10 bogies. ETH 6X.

Notes:

10704 has Siemens bogies.
10734 was originally 2914 and used as a Royal Train staff sleeping car. It has 12 berths and a shower room and is ETH11X.

10647–10732. Lot No. 30961 Derby 1980–84. 43.5 t.
10734. Lot No. 31002 Derby/Wolverton 1985. 42.5 t.

10647	d		P		KT
10648	d*	**CS**	P	*SR*	IS
10649	d		P		KT
10650	d*	**CS**	P	*SR*	IS
10658	d		P		KT
10663	d		P		KT
10666	d*	**CS**	P	*SR*	IS
10675	d	**CS**	P	*SR*	IS
10680	d*	**CS**	P	*SR*	IS
10683	d	**CS**	P	*SR*	IS
10688	d	**CS**	P	*SR*	IS
10689	d	**CP**	P	*SR*	IS
10690	d	**CS**	P	*SR*	IS
10693	d	**CS**	P	*SR*	IS
10697	d		P		KT
10699	d*	**CS**	P	*SR*	IS
10701	d		P		KT
10703	d	**CS**	P	*SR*	IS
10704	d		AE		ZA
10706	d*	**CS**	P	*SR*	IS
10710	d		P		KT
10714	d*	**CS**	P	*SR*	IS
10718	d*	**CS**	P	*SR*	IS
10719	d*	**CS**	P	*SR*	IS

10722	d* **CS**	P	*SR*	IS	10732	d	P		KT
10723	d* **CS**	P	*SR*	IS	10734	**VN**	VS	*VS*	CP
10729	**VN**	VS	*VS*	CP					

AD1G (FO)   OPEN FIRST

Mark 3A. Air conditioned. All now refurbished with table lamps and new seat cushions and trim. 48/– 2T (* 48/– 1T 1TD). BT10 bogies. d. ETH 6X.

11005–7 were open composites 11905–7 for a time.

Non-standard Livery: 11039 is EWS dark maroon.

Lot No. 30878 Derby 1975–76. 34.3 t.

11005	**V**	P		LT	11031	**V**	P		WI
11006	**V**	P		LT	11033	**V**	P	*CD*	OY
11007	**V**	P		LT	11036	**V**	P	*E*	WB
11011 *	**V**	P		WI	11037	**V**	P		ZD
11013	**V**	P	*CD*	OY	11038	**1**	P		LT
11016	**V**	P	*E*	OM	11039	**0**	E	*E*	TO
11017	**V**	P		LT	11040	**V**	P		WI
11018	**V**	P		LT	11042	**V**	P		WI
11019	**V**	P	*E*	OM	11044	**V**	P	*1A*	NC
11020	**V**	P		WI	11045	**V**	P	*E*	OM
11021	**V**	P	*E*	OM	11046	**V**	P	*E*	OM
11023	**1**	P		LT	11048	**V**	P	*E*	WB
11024	**V**	P		PC	11052	**V**	P		WI
11026	**V**	P		WI	11054	**V**	P	*E*	OM
11027	**V**	P	*E*	WB	11055	**V**	P		LT
11028	**V**	P	*E*	OM	11058	**V**	P		LT
11029	**V**	P	*CD*	OY	11060	**V**	P		WI
11030	**V**	P	*E*	OM					

AD1H (FO)   OPEN FIRST

Mark 3B. Air conditioned. Inter-City 80 seats. All now refurbished with table lamps and new seat cushions and trim. 48/– 2T. BT10 bogies. d. ETH 6X.

Lot No. 30982 Derby 1985. 36.5 t.

11064	**V**	P	*E*	WB	11077	**V**	P	*1A*	NC
11065	**V**	P		PC	11078	**V**	P		ZD
11066	**V**	P		OY	11079	**V**	P	*E*	WB
11067	**V**	P	*1A*	NC	11080	**V**	P	*1A*	NC
11068	**V**	P		ZD	11081	**V**	P		ZD
11069	**V**	P		ZD	11082	**V**	P		ZD
11070	**V**	P		ZD	11083	**V**	P	*E*	WB
11071	**V**	P	*1A*	NC	11084	**V**	P	*1A*	NC
11072	**V**	P		ZD	11085	**V**	P		ZD
11073	**V**	P		ZD	11086	**V**	P		WB
11074	**V**	P	*1A*	NC	11087	**V**	P	*1A*	NC
11075	**1**	P	*1A*	NC	11088	**V**	P		ZD
11076	**1**	P	*1A*	NC	11089	**V**	P	*E*	OM

11090	**V**	P		ZD	11096	**V**	P		ZD
11091	**V**	P	1A	NC	11097	**V**	P	1A	NC
11092	**V**	P		ZD	11098	**V**	P		ZD
11093	**V**	P		ZD	11099	**V**	P		ZD
11094	**V**	P		ZD	11100	**V**	P		ZD
11095	**V**	P	1A	NC	11101	**V**	P		ZD

AD1J (FO)   OPEN FIRST

Mark 4. Air conditioned. All except vehicles marked * rebuilt with new interior by Bombardier Wakefield 2003–05 (some converted from standard class vehicles) and known as "Mallard" stock. 46/– 1T. BT41 bogies. ETH 6X.

Note: 11264–11271 were cancelled and 11296/7 replaced by 11998/9.

Lot No. 31046 Metro-Cammell 1989–92. 41.3 t. (39.7 t.*).

11201		**GN** H *GN* BN	11283	(12435)	**GN** H *GN* BN
11203	*	**GN** H *GN* BN	11284	(12487)	**GN** H *GN* BN
11216	*	**GN** H *GN* BN	11285	(12537)	**GN** H *GN* BN
11219		**GN** H *GN* BN	11286	(12482)	**GN** H *GN* BN
11229		**GN** H *GN* BN	11287	(12527)	**GN** H *GN* BN
11237		**GN** H *GN* BN	11288	(12517)	**GN** H *GN* BN
11241		**GN** H *GN* BN	11289	(12528)	**GN** H *GN* BN
11244		**GN** H *GN* BN	11290	(12530)	**GN** H *GN* BN
11273		**GN** H *GN* BN	11291	(12535)	**GN** H *GN* BN
11277	(12408)	**GN** H *GN* BN	11292	(12451)	**GN** H *GN* BN
11278	(12479)	**GN** H *GN* BN	11293	(12536)	**GN** H *GN* BN
11279	(12521)	**GN** H *GN* BN	11294	(12529)	**GN** H *GN* BN
11280	(12523)	**GN** H *GN* BN	11295	(12475)	**GN** H *GN* BN
11281	(12418)	**GN** H *GN* BN	11298	(12416)	**GN** H *GN* BN
11282	(12524)	**GN** H *GN* BN	11299	( )	

AD1J (FOD)   OPEN FIRST (DISABLED)

Mark 4. Air conditioned. "Mallard" vehicles. Rebuilt from FO by Bombardier Wakefield 2003–05. 42/– 1W 1TD. BT41 bogies. ETH 6X.

Lot No. 31046 Metro-Cammell 1989–92. 40.7 t.

11301	(11215)	**GN** H *GN* BN	11314	(11207)	**GN** H *GN* BN
11302	( )	**GN** H	11315	(11238)	**GN** H *GN* BN
11303	(11211)	**GN** H *GN* BN	11316	(11227)	**GN** H *GN* BN
11304	(11257)	**GN** H *GN* BN	11317	(11223)	**GN** H *GN* BN
11305	(11261)	**GN** H *GN* BN	11318	(11251)	**GN** H *GN* BN
11306	(11276)	**GN** H *GN* BN	11319	(11247)	**GN** H *GN* BN
11307	(11217)	**GN** H *GN* BN	11320	(11255)	**GN** H *GN* BN
11308	(11263)	**GN** H *GN* BN	11321	(11245)	**GN** H *GN* BM
11309	(11259)	**GN** H *GN* BN	11322	(11228)	**GN** H *GN* BN
11310	(11272)	**GN** H *GN* BN	11323	(11235)	**GN** H *GN* BN
11311	(11221)	**GN** H *GN* BN	11324	(11253)	**GN** H *GN* BN
11312	(11225)	**GN** H *GN* BN	11325	(11231)	**GN** H *GN* BM
11313	(11210)	**GN** H *GN* BN	11326	(11206)	**GN** H *GN* BN

| 11327 (11236) | **GN** H *GN* BN | 11329 (11243) | **GN** H *GN* BN |
| 11328 (11274) | **GN** H *GN* BN | 11330 (11249) | **GN** H *GN* BN |

AD1J (FOS)   OPEN FIRST (SMOKING)

Mark 4. Air conditioned. "Mallard" vehicles. Rebuilt from FO by Bombardier Wakefield 2003–05. 46/– 1W 1TD. Partitioned off area for 7 smokers. BT41 bogies. ETH 6X.

Lot Nos. 31046/31049 Metro-Cammell 1989–92. 42.1 t.

11401 (11214)	**GN** H *GN* BN	11416 (11254)	**GN** H *GN* BN
11402 ( )	**GN** H	11417 (11226)	**GN** H *GN* BN
11403 (11258)	**GN** H *GN* BN	11418 (11222)	**GN** H *GN* BN
11404 (11202)	**GN** H *GN* BN	11419 (11250)	**GN** H *GN* BN
11405 (11204)	**GN** H *GN* BN	11420 (11242)	**GN** H *GN* BN
11406 (11205)	**GN** H *GN* BN	11421 (11220)	**GN** H *GN* BN
11407 (11256)	**GN** H *GN* BN	11422 (11232)	**GN** H *GN* BN
11408 (11218)	**GN** H *GN* BN	11423 (11230)	**GN** H *GN* BN
11409 (11262)	**GN** H *GN* BN	11424 (11239)	**GN** H *GN* BN
11410 (11260)	**GN** H *GN* BN	11425 (11234)	**GN** H *GN* BN
11411 (11240)	**GN** H *GN* BN	11426 (11252)	**GN** H *GN* BN
11412 (11209)	**GN** H *GN* BN	11427 (11200)	**GN** H *GN* BN
11413 (11212)	**GN** H *GN* BN	11428 (11233)	**GN** H *GN* BN
11414 (11246)	**GN** H *GN* BN	11429 (11275)	**GN** H *GN* BN
11415 (11208)	**GN** H *GN* BN	11430 (11248)	**GN** H *GN* BN

AD1J (FO)   OPEN FIRST

Mark 4. Air conditioned. 46/– 1T. BT41 bogies. ETH 6X. "Mallard" vehicles. Converted from TFRB with new interior Bombardier Wakefield 2005.

Lot No. 31046 Metro-Cammell 1989–92. 41.3 t.

| 11998 (10314) | **GN** H *GN* BN | 11999 (10316) | **GN** H *GN* BN |

AC2G (TSO)   OPEN STANDARD

Mark 3A. Air conditioned. All refurbished with modified seat backs and new layout and further refurbished with new seat trim. –/76 2T (s –/70 2T 2W, z –/70 1TD 1T 2W). BT10 bogies. d. ETH 6X.

t Coaches modified for One Anglia with 8 Compin Pegasus seats at saloon ends for "priority" use and more unidirectional seating. –/80 2T.

Note: 12169–72 were converted from open composites 11908–10/22, formerly FOs 11008–10/22.

Lot No. 30877 Derby 1975–77. 34.3 t.

12004	**V** P	WI	12010	**V** P	PC
12005	**V** P *1A*	NC	12011	**V** P *E*	WB
12007	**V** P	WI	12012	**V** P *1A*	NC
12008	**V** P	WI	12013	**V** P	ZD
12009	**V** P	ZD	12014	**V** P *SR*	PC

12015	V	P		ZD
12016	V	P		ZD
12017	V	P		WI
12019	V	P		ZD
12020	V	P		ZD
12021	V	P	1A	NC
12022	V	P		WI
12023	V	P		ZD
12024 s	V	P		ZD
12025	V	P		WI
12026	V	P		ZD
12027	V	P		ZD
12028	V	P		PC
12029	V	P		WI
12030	V	P		ZD
12031	V	P		ZD
12032	V	P		ZD
12033 z	V	P	1A	NC
12034	V	P		ZD
12035	V	P	1A	NC
12036 s	V	P		WI
12037 t	1	P	1A	NC
12038	V	P	SR	PC
12040	V	P		ZD
12041	V	P		ZD
12042 s	V	P		ZD
12043	V	P	E	WB
12044	V	P	1A	NC
12045	V	P	SR	PC
12046	V	P		PC
12047 z	V	P		WI
12048	V	P	IA	NC
12049	V	P		ZD
12050 s	V	P		WI
12051	V	P	1A	NC
12052	V	P	CD	OY
12053	V	P	E	WB
12054 s	V	P	E	WB
12055	V	P		WI
12056	V	P		ZD
12057	V	P		ZD
12058	V	P	1A	NC
12059 s	V	P		WI
12060	V	P		ZD
12061 s	V	P	1A	NC
12062 t	1	P	1A	NC
12063	V	P	E	WB
12064	V	P	1A	NC
12065	V	P	SR	PC
12066	V	P		PC
12067	V	P		PC
12068	V	P	SR	PC
12069	V	P	E	WB
12070	V	P	CD	OY
12071	V	P		WI
12072	V	P		WI
12073	V	P		ZD
12075	V	P		WB
12076	V	P		WI
12077	V	P	CD	OY
12078	V	P	E	WB
12079	1	P	1A	NC
12080	V	P		WI
12081	V	P		ZD
12082	1	P		ZD
12083	V	P		WI
12084	V	P		ZD
12085 s	V	P	SR	PC
12086 s	V	P		WI
12087 s	V	P		WI
12088 z	1	P	CD	OY
12089	V	P	1A	NC
12090	V	P		ZD
12091	V	P		ZD
12092	V	P	SR	PC
12093	V	P		ZD
12094	V	P	1A	NC
12095	V	P		WI
12096	V	P		PC
12097	V	P		ZD
12098	V	P	1A	NC
12099	V	P		ZD
12100 z	V	P	SR	PC
12101 s	V	P		WB
12102	V	P		WB
12103 s	1	P	1A	NC
12104	V	P		WB
12105 t	1	P	1A	NC
12106	V	P		WI
12107	V	P		ZD
12108 s	V	P		ZD
12109 t	1	P	1A	NC
12110	V	P		OY
12111	V	P		ZD
12112 z	V	P	1A	NC
12113	V	P		WI
12114	V	P		ZD
12115	V	P		ZD
12116	1	P		ZD
12117	V	P	E	WB
12118	V	P		ZD
12119	V	P	E	WB

12120	V	P		ZD
12121	V	P		WB
12122 z	V	P		PC
12123	V	P	1A	NC
12124	V	P		OY
12125	V	P	1A	NC
12126	V	P	1A	NC
12127	V	P	1A	NC
12128 s	V	P	SR	PC
12129	V	P	CD	OY
12130	V	P	1A	NC
12131	V	P		WB
12132	V	P	1A	NC
12133	V	P	E	WB
12134	V	P		WI
12135	V	P		OY
12136	V	P	1A	NC
12137	V	P		ZD
12138	V	P	E	WB
12139	V	P	SR	PC
12141	V	P	1A	NC
12142 z	V	P	1A	NC
12143	V	P		ZD
12144 s	V	P		WI
12145	V	P		WB
12146	V	P		ZD
12147	V	P	SR	PC
12148	1	P		ZD
12149	V	P		WB
12150	V	P		WB
12151	V	P		WB
12152	V	P	1A	NC
12153	V	P		ZD
12154	1	P		ZD
12155 s	V	P	1A	NC
12156	V	P		WI
12157	V	P	1A	NC
12158	V	P	1A	NC
12159	V	P		ZD
12160 s	V	P		WI
12161 z	V	P	E	WB
12163	V	P		WI
12164	V	P		WB
12165	V	P		WB
12166	V	P		ZD
12167	V	P	1A	NC
12168 s	V	P		ZD
12169 s	V	P		WI
12170 s	V	P		ZD
12171 s	V	P		ZD
12172 s	V	P	SR	PC

AI2J (TSOE) OPEN STANDARD (END)

Mark 4. Air conditioned. All except vehicles marked * rebuilt with new interior by Bombardier Wakefield 2003–05 and known as "Mallard" stock. Partitioned off area for 26 smokers (although smoking now banned!) –/76 1T. BT41 bogies. ETH 6X.

Lot No. 31047 Metro-Cammell 1989–91. 39.5 t.

Note: 12232 was converted from the original 12405.

12200	GN	H	GN	BN	12217	GN	H	GN	BN
12201	GN	H	GN	BN	12218	GN	H	GN	BN
12202	GN	H	GN	BN	12219	GN	H	GN	BN
12203	GN	H	GN	BN	12220	GN	H	GN	BN
12204	GN	H	GN	BN	12222	GN	H	GN	BN
12205	GN	H	GN	BN	12223	GN	H	GN	BN
12207	GN	H	GN	BN	12224	GN	H	GN	BN
12208	GN	H	GN	BN	12225	GN	H	GN	BN
12209	GN	H	GN	BN	12226	GN	H	GN	BN
12210	GN	H	GN	BN	12227	GN	H	GN	BN
12211	GN	H	GN	BN	12228	GN	H	GN	BN
12212	GN	H	GN	BN	12229	GN	H	GN	BN
12213	GN	H	GN	BN	12230	GN	H	GN	BN
12214	GN	H	GN	BN	12231	GN	H	GN	BN
12215	GN	H	GN	BN	12232 *	GN	H	GN	BN
12216	GN	H	GN	BN					

AL2J (TSOD) OPEN STANDARD (DISABLED ACCESS)

Mark 4. Air conditioned. All except vehicles marked * rebuilt with new interior by Bombardier Wakefield 2003–05 and known as "Mallard" stock. –/68 2W 1TD. (–/72 1W 1TD*). BT41 bogies. ETH 6X.

Note: 12331 has been converted from 12531.

Lot No. 31048 Metro-Cammell 1989–91. 39.4 t.

12300		**GN**	H *GN*	BN	12317	**GN**	H *GN*	BN
12301		**GN**	H *GN*	BN	12318	**GN**	H *GN*	BN
12302	*	**GN**	H *GN*	BN	12319	**GN**	H *GN*	BN
12303		**GN**	H *GN*	BN	12320	**GN**	H *GN*	BN
12304		**GN**	H *GN*	BN	12321	**GN**	H *GN*	BN
12305		**GN**	H *GN*	BN	12322	**GN**	H *GN*	BN
12307		**GN**	H *GN*	BN	12323	**GN**	H *GN*	BN
12308		**GN**	H *GN*	BN	12324	**GN**	H *GN*	BN
12309		**GN**	H *GN*	BN	12325	**GN**	H *GN*	BN
12310		**GN**	H *GN*	BN	12326	**GN**	H *GN*	BN
12311		**GN**	H *GN*	BN	12327	**GN**	H *GN*	BN
12312		**GN**	H *GN*	BN	12328	**GN**	H *GN*	BN
12313		**GN**	H *GN*	BN	12329	**GN**	H *GN*	BN
12315		**GN**	H *GN*	BN	12330	**GN**	H *GN*	BN
12316		**GN**	H *GN*	BN	12331	**GN**	H *GN*	BN

AC2J (TSO)   OPEN STANDARD

Mark 4. Air conditioned. All except vehicles marked * rebuilt with new interior by Bombardier Wakefield 2003–05 and known as "Mallard" stock. –/74 2T. BT41 bogies. ETH 6X.

Lot No. 31049 Metro-Cammell 1989–92. 39.9 t. (40.8 t. m).

Note: 12405 is the second coach to carry that number. It was built from the bodyshell originally intended for 12221. The original 12405 is now 12232. 12490–12512 were cancelled.

12400		**GN**	H *GN*	BN	12420	**GN**	H *GN*	BN
12401		**GN**	H *GN*	BN	12421	**GN**	H *GN*	BN
12402	*	**GN**	H *GN*	BN	12422	**GN**	H *GN*	BN
12403		**GN**	H *GN*	BN	12423	**GN**	H *GN*	BN
12404		**GN**	H *GN*	BN	12424	**GN**	H *GN*	BN
12405		**GN**	H *GN*	BN	12425	**GN**	H *GN*	BN
12406		**GN**	H *GN*	BN	12426	**GN**	H *GN*	BN
12407		**GN**	H *GN*	BN	12427	**GN**	H *GN*	BN
12409		**GN**	H *GN*	BN	12428	**GN**	H *GN*	BN
12410		**GN**	H *GN*	BN	12429	**GN**	H *GN*	BN
12411		**GN**	H *GN*	BN	12430	**GN**	H *GN*	BN
12414		**GN**	H *GN*	BN	12431	**GN**	H *GN*	BN
12415		**GN**	H *GN*	BN	12432	**GN**	H *GN*	BN
12417		**GN**	H *GN*	BN	12433	**GN**	H *GN*	BN
12419		**GN**	H *GN*	BN	12434	**GN**	H *GN*	BN

12436	**GN**	H *GN*	BN		12468	**GN**	H *GN*	BN
12437	**GN**	H *GN*	BN		12469	**GN**	H *GN*	BN
12438	**GN**	H *GN*	BN		12470	**GN**	H *GN*	BN
12439	**GN**	H *GN*	BN		12471	**GN**	H *GN*	BN
12440	**GN**	H *GN*	BN		12472	**GN**	H *GN*	BN
12441	**GN**	H *GN*	BN		12473	**GN**	H *GN*	BN
12442	**GN**	H *GN*	BN		12474	**GN**	H *GN*	BN
12443	**GN**	H *GN*	BN		12476	**GN**	H *GN*	BN
12444	**GN**	H *GN*	BN		12477	**GN**	H *GN*	BN
12445	**GN**	H *GN*	BN		12478	**GN**	H *GN*	BN
12446	**GN**	H *GN*	BN		12480	**GN**	H *GN*	BN
12447	**GN**	H *GN*	BN		12481	**GN**	H *GN*	BN
12448 *	**GN**	H *GN*	BN		12483	**GN**	H *GN*	BN
12449	**GN**	H *GN*	BN		12484	**GN**	H *GN*	BN
12450 *	**GN**	H *GN*	BN		12485	**GN**	H *GN*	BN
12452	**GN**	H *GN*	BN		12486	**GN**	H *GN*	BN
12453	**GN**	H *GN*	BN		12488	**GN**	H *GN*	BN
12454	**GN**	H *GN*	BN		12489	**GN**	H *GN*	BN
12455	**GN**	H *GN*	BN		12513	**GN**	H *GN*	BN
12456	**GN**	H *GN*	BN		12514	**GN**	H *GN*	BN
12457	**GN**	H *GN*	BN		12515	**GN**	H *GN*	BN
12458	**GN**	H *GN*	BN		12518	**GN**	H *GN*	BN
12459	**GN**	H *GN*	BN		12519	**GN**	H *GN*	BN
12460	**GN**	H *GN*	BN		12520	**GN**	H *GN*	BN
12461	**GN**	H *GN*	BN		12522	**GN**	H *GN*	BN
12462	**GN**	H *GN*	BN		12526	**GN**	H *GN*	BN
12463	**GN**	H *GN*	BN		12532 *	**GN**	H *GN*	BN
12464	**GN**	H *GN*	BN		12533	**GN**	H *GN*	BN
12465	**GN**	H *GN*	BN		12534	**GN**	H *GN*	BN
12466	**GN**	H *GN*	BN		12538	**GN**	H *GN*	BN
12467	**GN**	H *GN*	BN					

AA11 (FK)   CORRIDOR FIRST

Mark 1. 42/– 2T. ETH 3.

13229–13230. Lot No. 30381 Swindon 1959. B4 bogies. 33 t.
13321. Lot No. 30667 Swindon 1962. Commonwealth bogies. 36 t.

| 13229 | xk | **M** | BK *BK* | BT | | 13321 | x | **M** | WC | CS |
| 13230 | xk | **M** | BK *BK* | BT | | | | | | |

AA1A (FK)   CORRIDOR FIRST

Mark 2A. Pressure ventilated. 42/– 2T. B4 bogies. ETH 4.

13440. Lot No. 30774 Derby 1968. 33 t.
13474. Lot No. 30785 Derby 1968. 33 t.

| 13440 | v | **G** | FM *FM* | RL | | 13474 | v | **G** | FM *FM* | RL |

AD1B (FO)   OPEN FIRST

Mark 2B. Pressure ventilated. 42/– 2T. B4 bogies. ETH 4.

Lot No. 30789 Derby 1968. 33 t.

These two vehicles were built as FKs, sold to Northern Ireland Railways 1980 and regauged to 5'3". NIR converted them to 56-seater TSOs. Since withdrawn, repatriated to Britain and converted back to standard gauge 2002/3. Under conversion to FO.

13498 (13498, NIR926)	**PC**	RA		CS
13508 (13508, NIR924)	**PC**	RA		CS

AB11 (BFK)   CORRIDOR BRAKE FIRST

Mark 1. 24/– 1T. Commonwealth bogies. ETH 2.

14007. Lot No. 30382 Swindon 1959. 35 t.
17013–17019. Lot No. 30668 Swindon 1961. 36 t.
17023. Lot No. 30718 Swindon 1963. Metal window frames. 36 t.

Originally numbered in 14xxx series and then renumbered in 17xxx series.

14007	x	**M**	B1	*LS*	BH		17018	v	**CH**	VT	*VT*	TM
17013		**PC**	JH	*LS*	SO		17019	x	**M**	NE	*LS*	BQ
17015	x	**G**	E	*E*	OM		17023	x	**G**	E		BN

AB1Z (BFK)   CORRIDOR BRAKE FIRST

Mark 2. Pressure ventilated. 24/– 1T. B4 bogies. ETH 4.

Lot No. 30756 Derby 1966. 31.5 t.

Originally numbered 14041.

17041	**M**	DG	*LS*	BQ

AB1A (BFK)   CORRIDOR BRAKE FIRST

Mark 2A. Pressure ventilated. 24/– 1T. B4 bogies. ETH 4.

17056–17077. Lot No. 30775 Derby 1967–8. 32 t.
17086–17102. Lot No. 30786 Derby 1968. 32 t.

Originally numbered 14056–102. 17089 and 17090 were numbered 35502 and 35503 for a time when declassified.

17056		**CH**	RV	*RV*	CP		17090	v	**CH**	H		TM
17077		**RV**	RV	*RV*	CP		17096		**G**	MN	*LS*	SL
17086		**RV**	RV		CD		17102		**M**	WC	*WC*	CS
17089	v	**G**	FM		RL							

AX5B   COUCHETTE/GENERATOR COACH

Mark 2B. Formerly part of Royal Train. Converted from a BFK built 1969. Consists of luggage accommodation, guard's compartment, 350 kW diesel generator and staff sleeping accommodation. Pressure ventilated. B5 bogies. ETH 5X.

Non-standard Livery: 17105 is Oxford blue.

Lot No. 30888 Wolverton 1977. 46 t.

17105 (14105, 2905)	**O**	RV	*RV*	CP

AB1D (BFK)   CORRIDOR BRAKE FIRST

Mark 2D. Air conditioned (Stones equipment). 24/– 1T. B4 Bogies. ETH 5.

Lot No. 30823 Derby 1971–72. 33.5 t.

Non-Standard Livery: 17141 is purple.

Originally numbered 14141–72.

17141	**O**	E		FP	17165		E	FP
17144		FM		BH	17167	**VN**	VS	*VS*	CP
17153	**WR**	E		CS	17168 d	**M**	WC	*WC*	CS
17156		MA		DY	17169		E		CS
17159	**CH**	RV		SL	17170		FM		BH
17161		E		OM	17172		E		FP
17163		VS		CO					

AE1G (BFO)   OPEN BRAKE FIRST

Mark 3B. Air conditioned. Fitted with hydraulic handbrake. Refurbished with table lamps and burgundy seat trim. 36/– 1T (w 35/– 1T) BT10 bogies. pg. d. ETH 5X.

Lot No. 30990 Derby 1986. 35.81 t.

17173		**V**	P	*CD*	OY	17175 w	**V**	P		LT
17174		**V**	P	*CD*	OY					

AA21 (SK)   CORRIDOR STANDARD

Mark 1. Each vehicle has eight compartments. All remaining vehicles have metal window frames and melamine interior panelling. Commonwealth bogies. –/48 2T. ETH 4.

Lot No. 30685 Derby 1961–62. 36 t.

t Rebuilt internally as TSO using components from 4936. –/64 2T.

Originally numbered 25756–25893.

18756	x	**M**	WC	*WC*	CS	18808	x	**M**	WC	*WC*	CS
18767	x	**M**	WC	*WC*	CS	18862	x	**M**	WC	*WC*	CS
18806	xt	**M**	WC	*WC*	CS	18893	x	**CH**	WC		CS

AB31 (BCK)   CORRIDOR BRAKE COMPOSITE

Mark 1. There are two variants depending upon whether the standard class compartments have armrests. Each vehicle has two first and three standard class compartments. 12/18 2T (12/24 2T *). ETH 2.

21232. Lot No. 30574 GRCW 1960. B4 bogies. 34 t.
21241–21246. Lot No. 30669 Swindon 1961–62. Commonwealth bogies. 36 t.
21256. Lot No. 30731 Derby 1963. Commonwealth bogies. 37 t.
21266–21272. Lot No. 30732 Derby 1964. Commonwealth bogies. 37 t.

Non-Standard Livery: 21232 is in BR Carmine & Cream lined out in black and gold.

21232	x	**0**	62	*LS*	SK		21266	x*	**M**	WC *WC*	CS
21241	x	**M**	BK	*BK*	BT		21268	*		BS	SO
21245	x	**M**	E	*E*	OM		21269	*	**GC**	E *E*	OM
21246		**BG**	E	*E*	OM		21272	x*	**CH**	RV *RV*	CP
21256	x	**M**	WC	*WC*	CS						

AB21 (BSK)   CORRIDOR BRAKE STANDARD

Mark 1. There are two variants depending upon whether the compartments have armrests. Each vehicle has four compartments. Lots 30699 and 30721 have metal window frames and melamine interior panelling. –/24 1T. ETH2.

g Fitted with an e.t.s. generator.

35185. Lot No. 30427 Wolverton 1959. B4 bogies. 33 t.
35317–35333. Lot No. 30699 Wolverton 1962–63. Commonwealth bogies. 37 t.
35452–35486. Lot No. 30721 Wolverton 1963. Commonwealth bogies. 37 t.

Non-Standard Livery: 35465 is in BR Carmine & Cream lined out in black and gold.

35185	x	**M**	BK *BK*	BT		35463	v	**M**	WC *LS*	CS
35317	x	**G**	IR *LS*	BQ		35465	x	**0**	LW *LS*	CP
35329	v	**G**	MH *LS*	RL		35468	v	**M**	NM *LS*	YK
35333	x	**CH**	24 *LS*	DI		35469	xg	**M**	E *E*	OM
35452	x	**RR**	LW	CP		35470	v	**CH**	VT *LS*	TM
35453	x	**CH**	GW *LS*	DI		35476	x	**M**	62 *LS*	SK
35459	x	**M**	WC *WC*	CS		35479	v	**M**	SV *LS*	KR
35461	x	**CH**	RV *LS*	OM		35486	x	**M**	SV *LS*	KR

AB1C (BFK)   CORRIDOR BRAKE FIRST

Mark 2C. Pressure ventilated. Renumbered when declassified. –/24 1T. B4 bogies. ETH 4.

Lot No. 30796 Derby 1969–70. 32.5 t.

35508	(14128, 17128)	**M**	IR	*LS*	BQ

AB5C   BRAKE/POWER KITCHEN

Mark 2C. Pressure ventilated. Converted from BFK (declassified to BSK) built 1970. Converted at West Coast Railway Company 2000–01. Consists of 60 kVA generator, guard's compartment and electric kitchen. B5 bogies. ETH 4.

Non-Standard Livery: British Racing Green with gold lining.

Lot No. 30796 Derby 1969–70. 32.5 t.

35511	(14130, 17130)	**0**	RA		CP

AB1A (BFK)   CORRIDOR BRAKE FIRST

Mark 2A. Pressure ventilated. Renumbered when declassified. –/24 1T. B4 bogies. Cage removed from brake compartment. ETH 4.

Lot No. 30786 Derby 1968. 32 t.

35517	(14088, 17088)	**M**	IR	*LS*	BQ
35518	(14097, 17097)	**PC**	IR	*LS*	BQ

NAMED COACHES

The following miscellaneous coaches carry names:

1200	AMBER	3247	CHATSWORTH
1659	CAMELOT	3267	BELVOIR
1800	TINTAGEL	3273	ALNWICK
3105	JULIA	3275	HARLECH
3113	JESSICA	5193	CLAN MACLEOD
3117	CHRISTINA	5212	CAPERKAILZIE
3128	VICTORIA	5229	THE GREEN KNIGHT
3130	PAMELA	5239	THE RED KNIGHT
3136	DIANA	5278	MELISANDE
3143	PATRICIA	5350	Dawn
3174	GLAMIS	5365	Deborah
3181	TOPAZ	5376	Michaela
3182	WARWICK	5419	SIR LAUNCELOT
3188	ONYX	9391	PENDRAGON
3223	DIAMOND	10569	LEVIATHAN
3228	AMETHYST	10729	CREWE
3229	JADE	10734	BALMORAL
3231	Apollo	17013	ALBANNACH SGIATHACH
3240	SAPPHIRE	17086	Georgina
3244	EMERALD	35518	MERLIN

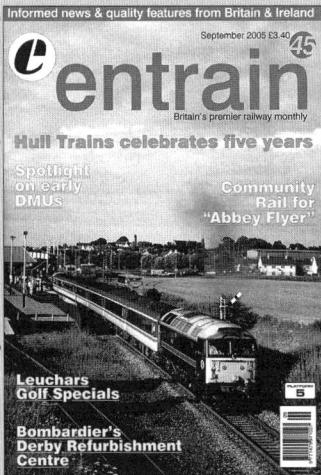

2. HIGH SPEED TRAIN TRAILER CARS

HSTs consist of a number of trailer cars (usually seven to nine) with a power car at each end. All trailer cars are classified Mark 3 and have BT10 bogies with disc brakes and central door locking. Heating is by a 415 V three-phase supply and vehicles have air conditioning. Max. Speed is 125 m.p.h.

All vehicles underwent a mid-life refurbishment in the 1980s, and a further refurbishment programme was completed in November 2000, with each train operating company having a different scheme as follows:

First Great Western. Green seat covers and extra partitions between seat bays.

Great North Eastern Railway. New ceiling lighting panels and brown seat covers. First class vehicles have table lamps and imitation walnut plastic end panels.

Virgin Cross-Country. Green seat covers. Standard class vehicles had four seats in the centre of each carriage replaced with a luggage stack. All have now passed to other operators or are in store.

Midland Mainline. Grey seat covers, redesigned seat squabs, side carpeting and two seats in the centre of each standard class carriage and one in first class carriages replaced with a luggage stack.

Midland Mainline vehicles underwent a further refurbishment programme during 2003/04. This involved fitting new fluorescent and halogen ceiling lighting and a new design of seat squab with blue upholstery in first class.

In addition, **GNER** buffet cars have been modernised with new corner bars and each set had an extra vehicle added with a disabled persons toilet.

Ten sets ex-Virgin Cross-Country, and some spare vehicles, were temporarily allocated to Midland Mainline for the temporary service to Manchester during 2003/04 and had a facelift. Buffet cars were converted from TRSB to TRFB and renumbered in the 408xx series. Midland Mainline retains one of these sets whilst the others are in use with First Great Western, GNER, Virgin XC (summer fleet) or are in store.

Tops Type Codes

TOPS type codes for HST trailer cars are made up as follows:

(1) Two letters denoting the layout of the vehicle as follows:

GH	Open	GL Kitchen
GJ	Open with Guard's compartment.	GN Buffet
GK	Buffet	

(2) A digit for the class of passenger accommodation

1	First	4 Unclassified
2	Standard (formerly second)	

(3) A suffix relating to the build of coach.

G   Mark 3

Operator Codes

The normal operator codes are given in brackets after the TOPS codes. These are as follows:

TF	Trailer First		TGS	Trailer Guard's Standard
TRB	Trailer Buffet First		TRSB	Trailer Buffet Standard
TRFB	Trailer Buffet First		TS	Trailer Standard

GN4G (TRB)   TRAILER BUFFET FIRST

Converted from TRSB by fitting first class seats. Renumbered from 404xx series by subtracting 200. 23/–.

40204–40228. Lot No. 30883 Derby 1976–77. 36.12 t.
40231. Lot No. 30899 Derby 1978–79. 36.12 t.

40204	**FG**	A	*GW*	PM		40210	**FG**	A	*GW*	PM
40205	**FG**	A	*GW*	PM		40221	**FG**	A	*GW*	PM
40207	**FG**	A	*GW*	PM		40228	**FG**	A	*GW*	PM
40208	**FG**	A	*GW*	PM		40231	**FG**	A	*GW*	PM
40209	**FG**	A	*GW*	PM						

GK2G (TRSB)   TRAILER BUFFET STANDARD

Renumbered from 400xx series by adding 400. –/33 1W.

40401–40426. Lot No. 30883 Derby 1976–77. 36.12 t.
40433–40437. Lot No. 30899 Derby 1978–79. 36.12 t.

Notes: 40433–40434 were numbered 40233–40234 for a time when fitted with 23 first class seats.

§ Experimentally refurbished First Group vehicle. Converted to TRFB. 23/–.

Non-standard livery: 40423 – First Group experimental (indigo, purple and blue with pink, white and blue stripes).

40401	**V**	FG		BR		40424	**V**	P		BR
40402	**V**	P		BR		40425	**V**	P		BR
40403	**V**	P		BR		40426	**V**	P		BR
40416	**V**	P		BR		40433	**V**	P		BR
40417	**V**	P		BR		40434	**V**	P		BR
40419	**V**	P		BR		40436	**GN**	P	*GN*	EC
40422	**V**	FG		LA		40437	**V**	FG		BR
40423 §	**0**	FG		SW						

GK1G (TRFB)   TRAILER BUFFET FIRST

These vehicles have larger kitchens than the 402xx and 404xx series vehicles, and are used in trains where full meal service is required. They were renumbered from the 403xx series (in which the seats were unclassified) by adding 400 to the previous number. 17/–.

40700–40721. Lot No. 30921 Derby 1978–79. 38.16 t.
40722–40735. Lot No. 30940 Derby 1979–80. 38.16 t.

40736–40753. Lot No. 30948 Derby 1980–81. 38.16 t.
40754–40757. Lot No. 30966 Derby 1982. 38.16 t.

r Modified with new corner bar.

40700	**MN**	P	*MM*	NL	40730	**MN**	P	*MM*	NL
40701	**MN**	P	*MM*	NL	40731	**FG**	A	*GW*	LA
40702	**MN**	P	*MM*	NL	40732 ✓	**MN**	A	*MM*	NL
40703	**FG**	A	*GW*	LA	40733	**FG**	A	*GW*	LA
40704 r	**GN**	A	*GN*	EC	40734	**FG**	A	*GW*	LA
40705 r	**GN**	A	*GN*	EC	40735 r	**GN**	A	*GN*	EC
40706 r	**GN**	A	*GN*	EC	40736	**FG**	A	*GW*	LA
40707	**FG**	A	*GW*	LA	40737 r	**GN**	A	*GN*	EC
40708	**MN**	P	*MM*	NL	40738	**FG**	A	*GW*	LA
40709	**FG**	A	*GW*	LA	40739	**FG**	A	*GW*	PM
40710	**FG**	A	*GW*	LA	40740 r	**GN**	A	*GN*	EC
40711 r	**GN**	A	*GN*	EC	40741	**MN**	P	*MM*	NL
40712	**FG**	A	*GW*	LA	40742 r	**GN**	A	*GN*	EC
40713	**FG**	A	*GW*	LA	40743	**FG**	A	*GW*	LA
40714	**FG**	A	*GW*	PM	40744	**FG**	A	*GW*	LA
40715	**FG**	A	*GW*	LA	40745	**FG**	A	*GW*	LA
40716	**FG**	A	*GW*	PM	40746	**MN**	P	*MM*	NL
40717	**FG**	A	*GW*	LA	40747	**FG**	A	*GW*	PM
40718	**FG**	A	*GW*	LA	40748 r	**GN**	A	*GN*	EC
40720 r	**GN**	A	*GN*	EC	40749	**MN**	P	*MM*	NL
40721	**FG**	A	*GW*	LA	40750 r	**GN**	A	*GN*	EC
40722 ✓	**FG**	A	*GW*	LA	40751	**MN**	P	*MM*	NL
40723 ✓	**MN**	A	*MM*	NL	40752	**FG**	A	*GW*	LA
40724	**FG**	A	*GW*	LA	40753	**MN**	P	*MM*	NL
40725	**FG**	A	*GW*	LA	40754	**MN**	P	*MM*	NL
40726	**FG**	A	*GW*	LA	40755	**FG**	A	*GW*	LA
40727 ✓	**FG**	A	*GW*	LA	40756	**MN**	P	*MM*	NL
40728 ✓	**MN**	P	*MM*	NL	40757	**FG**	A	*GW*	LA
40729	**MN**	P	*MM*	NL					

GK1G (TRFB)   TRAILER BUFFET FIRST

These vehicles have been converted from TRSBs in the 404xx series to be similar to the 407xx series vehicles. 17/– .

40801–40803/40805/40808/40809/40811. Lot No. 30883 Derby 1976–77. 38.16 t.
40804/40806/40807/40810. Lot No. 30899 Derby 1978–79. 38.16 t.

Note: 40802/40804/40811 were numbered 40212/40232/40211 for a time when fitted with 23 first class seats.

40801	(40027, 40427)	**FG**	P	*GW*	LA
40802	(40012, 40412)	**FG**	P	*GW*	LA
40803	(40018, 40418)	**FG**	P	*GW*	LA
40804	(40032, 40432)	**MN**	P	*MM*	NL
40805	(40020, 40420)	**GN**	P	*GN*	EC
40806	(40029, 40429)	**FG**	P	*GW*	LA
40807	(40035, 40435)	**MN**	P	*MM*	NL

40808	(40015, 40415)	**FG**	P	*GW*	LA
40809	(40014, 40414)	**MN**	P	*VX*	NL
40810	(40030, 40430)	**MN**	P	*VX*	NL
40811	(40011, 40411)	**GN**	P	*GN*	EC

GH1G (TF)   TRAILER FIRST

41003–41056. Lot No. 30881 Derby 1976–77. 33.66 t.
41057–41120. Lot No. 30896 Derby 1977–78. 33.66 t.
41121–41148. Lot No. 30938 Derby 1979–80. 33.66 t.
41149–41166. Lot No. 30947 Derby 1980. 33.66 t.
41167–41169. Lot No. 30963 Derby 1982. 33.66 t.
41170. Lot No. 30967 Derby 1982. Former prototype vehicle. 33.66 t.
41179/41180. Lot No. 30884 Derby 1976–77. 33.66 t.
41181–41184/41189. Lot No. 30939 Derby 1979–80. 33.66 t.
41185–41188. Lot No. 30969 Derby 1982. 33.66 t.

As built 48/– 2T. (w 47/– 2T 1W).
s Fitted with centre luggage stack. 46/– 1T 1TD 1W.

41003		**FG**	A	*GW*	LA	41037		**FG**	A	*GW*	LA
41004		**FG**	A	*GW*	PM	41038		**FG**	A	*GW*	LA
41005		**FG**	A	*GW*	LA	41039		**GN**	A	*GN*	EC
41006		**FG**	A	*GW*	LA	41040	w	**GN**	A	*GN*	EC
41007		**FG**	A	*GW*	PM	41041	s	**MN**	P	*MM*	NL
41008		**FG**	A	*GW*	PM	41043		**GN**	A	*GN*	EC
41009		**FG**	A	*GW*	PM	41044	w	**GN**	A	*GN*	EC
41010		**FG**	A	*GW*	PM	41045	w	**V**		FG		BR
41011		**FG**	A	*GW*	PM	41046	s	**MN**	P	*MM*	NL
41012		**FG**	A	*GW*	PM	41051		**FG**	A	*GW*	LA
41015		**FG**	A	*GW*	PM	41052		**FG**	A	*GW*	LA
41016		**FG**	A	*GW*	PM	41055		**FG**	A	*GW*	LA
41017		**FG**	A	*GW*	PM	41056		**FG**	A	*GW*	LA
41018		**FG**	A	*GW*	PM	41057		**MN**	P	*MM*	NL
41019		**FG**	A	*GW*	PM	41058	s	**MN**	P	*MM*	NL
41020		**FG**	A	*GW*	PM	41059	w	**V**		FG		BR
41021		**FG**	A	*GW*	PM	41061		**MN**	P	*MM*	NL
41022		**FG**	A	*GW*	PM	41062	rw	**MN**	P	*MM*	NL
41023		**FG**	A	*GW*	LA	41063		**MN**	P	*MM*	NL
41024		**FG**	A	*GW*	LA	41064	s	**MN**	P	*MM*	NL
41025		**MN**	A	*MM*	NL	41065		**FG**	A	*GW*	LA
41026		**MN**	A	*MM*	NL	41066		**GN**	A	*GN*	EC
41027		**FG**	A	*GW*	LA	41067	s	**MN**	P	*MM*	NL
41028		**FG**	A	*GW*	LA	41068	s	**MN**	P	*MM*	NL
41029		**FG**	A	*GW*	LA	41069	s	**MN**	P	*MM*	NL
41030		**FG**	A	*GW*	LA	41070	s	**MN**	P	*MM*	NL
41031		**FG**	A	*GW*	LA	41071		**MN**	P	*MM*	NL
41032		**FG**	A	*GW*	LA	41072	s	**MN**	P	*MM*	NL
41033		**FG**	A	*GW*	LA	41075		**MN**	P	*MM*	NL
41034		**FG**	A	*GW*	LA	41076	s	**MN**	P	*MM*	NL
41035		**MN**	A	*MM*	NL	41077		**MN**	P	*MM*	NL
41036	w	**MN**	A	*MM*	NL	41078		**MN**	P	*MM*	NL

41079		**MN**	P	*MM*	NL	41125		**FG**	A	*GW*	LA
41080	s	**MN**	P	*MM*	NL	41126		**FG**	A	*GW*	LA
41081	w	**MN**	P	*MM*	NL	41127		**FG**	A	*GW*	LA
41083		**MN**	P	*MM*	NL	41128		**FG**	A	*GW*	LA
41084	s	**MN**	P	*MM*	NL	41129		**FG**	A	*GW*	PM
41085		**GN**	P	*GN*	EC	41130		**FG**	A	*GW*	PM
41086	w	**V**	FG		LA	41131		**FG**	A	*GW*	LA
41087		**GN**	A	*GN*	EC	41132		**FG**	A	*GW*	LA
41088	w	**GN**	A	*GN*	EC	41133		**FG**	A	*GW*	LA
41089		**FG**	A	*GW*	LA	41134		**FG**	A	*GW*	LA
41090	w	**GN**	A	*GN*	EC	41135		**FG**	A	*GW*	LA
41091		**GN**	A	*GN*	EC	41136		**FG**	A	*GW*	LA
41092	w	**GN**	A	*GN*	EC	41137		**FG**	A	*GW*	PM
41093		**FG**	A	*GW*	LA	41138		**FG**	A	*GW*	PM
41094		**FG**	A	*GW*	LA	41139		**FG**	A	*GW*	LA
41095	w	**GN**	P	*GN*	EC	41140		**FG**	A	*GW*	LA
41096	w	**MN**	P	*VX*	NL	41141		**FG**	A	*GW*	LA
41097		**GN**	A	*GN*	EC	41142		**FG**	A	*GW*	LA
41098	w	**GN**	A	*GN*	EC	41143		**FG**	A	*GW*	LA
41099		**GN**	A	*GN*	EC	41144		**FG**	A	*GW*	LA
41100	w	**GN**	A	*GN*	EC	41145		**FG**	A	*GW*	LA
41101		**FG**	A	*GW*	LA	41146		**FG**	A	*GW*	LA
41102		**FG**	A	*GW*	LA	41147	w	**FG**	P	*GW*	LA
41103		**FG**	A	*GW*	LA	41148	w	**V**	P		BR
41104		**FG**	A	*GW*	LA	41149	w	**FG**	P	*GW*	LA
41105		**FG**	A	*GW*	PM	41150	w	**GN**	A	*GN*	EC
41106		**FG**	A	*GW*	PM	41151		**GN**	A	*GN*	EC
41107	w	**FG**	P	*GW*	LA	41152		**GN**	A	*GN*	EC
41108	w	**MN**	P		NL	41153		**MN**	P	*MM*	NL
41109	w	**FG**	P	*GW*	LA	41154	s	**MN**	P	*MM*	NL
41110		**FG**	A	*GW*	PM	41155		**MN**	P	*MM*	NL
41111		**MN**	P	*MM*	NL	41156		**MN**	P	*MM*	NL
41112		**MN**	P	*MM*	NL	41157		**FG**	A	*GW*	LA
41113	s	**MN**	P	*MM*	NL	41158		**FG**	A	*GW*	LA
41114	w	**V**	FG		LA	41159	w	**V**	P		BR
41115	w	**V**	P		BR	41160	w	**V**	FG		LA
41116		**FG**	A	*GW*	LA	41161	w	**MN**	P		NL
41117		**MN**	P	*MM*	NL	41162	w	**V**	FG		LA
41118	w	**GN**	A	*GN*	EC	41163	w	**V**	FG		BR
41119	w	**MN**	P	*MM*	NL	41164	w	**GN**	A	*GN*	EC
41120		**GN**	A	*GN*	EC	41165	w	**V**	P		BR
41121		**FG**	A	*GW*	LA	41166	w	**V**	FG		BR
41122		**FG**	A	*GW*	LA	41167	w	**GN**	P	*GN*	EC
41123		**FG**	A	*GW*	PM	41168	w	**FG**	P	*GW*	LA
41124		**FG**	A	*GW*	PM	41169	w	**V**	P		BR

41170	(41001)	**GN**	A	*GN*	EC	41184	(42270)	**MN**	P	BR
41179	(40505)	**FG**	A	*GW*	PM	41185	(42313)	**GN**	P	*GN*	EC
41180	(40511)	**FG**	A	*GW*	LA	41186	(42312)	**FG**	P	*GW*	LA
41181	(42282)	**FG**	P	*GW*	LA	41187	(42311)	**MN**	P	NL
41182	(42278)	**FG**	P	*GW*	LA	41188	(42310)	**FG**	P	*GW*	LA
41183	(42274)	**FG**	P	*GW*	LA	41189	(42298)	**MN**	P	*VX*	NL

GH2G (TS)   TRAILER STANDARD

42003–42090/42362. Lot No. 30882 Derby 1976–77. 33.60 t.
42091–42250. Lot No. 30897 Derby 1977–79. 33.60 t.
42251–42305. Lot No. 30939 Derby 1979–80. 33.60 t.
42306–42322. Lot No. 30969 Derby 1982. 33.60 t.
42323–42341. Lot No. 30983 Derby 1984–85. 33.60 t.
42342/42360. Lot No. 30949 Derby 1982. 33.47 t. Converted from TGS.
42343/42345. Lot No. 30970 Derby 1982. 33.47 t. Converted from TGS.
42344/42361. Lot No. 30964 Derby 1982. 33.47 t. Converted from TGS.
42346/42347/42350/42351. Lot No. 30881 Derby 1976–77. 33.66 t. Converted from TF.
42348/42349/42363. Lot No. 30896 Derby 1977–78. 33.66 t. Converted from TF.
42352/42354. Lot No. 30897 Derby 1977. Were TF from 1983 to 1992. 33.66 t.
42353/42355–42357. Lot No. 30967 Derby 1982. Ex-prototype vehicles. 33.66 t.

As built –/76 2T.
s Centre luggage stack –/72 2T.
t Centre luggage stack –/72 2T. Fitted with pt.
u Centre luggage stack –/74 2T.
w Centre luggage stack –72 2T 1W.
z Seats removed for wheelchair spaces –/70 2T 2W.
* disabled persons toilet and 5 tip-up seats. –/65 1T 1TD.
† disabled persons toilet. –/62 1T 1TD 1W.
e Rebuilt VOLO TV "entertainment" coach with new seats and on-train entertainment systems. 36 seats have monitors fixed to the seatbacks.
§ Experimentally refurbished First Group vehicle.

42158 was also numbered 41177 for a time when fitted with first class seats.

Non-standard liveries: 42076 – VOLO TV (all over silver with various images). 42353 – First Group experimental (indigo, purple and blue with pink, white and blue stripes).

42003		**FG**	A	*GW*	PM	42016	**FG**	A	*GW*	PM
42004	*	**FG**	A	*GW*	LA	42019	**FG**	A	*GW*	PM
42005		**FG**	A	*GW*	PM	42021	*	**FG**	A	*GW*	PM
42006		**FG**	A	*GW*	PM	42023	**FG**	A	*GW*	PM
42007	*	**FG**	A	*GW*	LA	42024	*	**FG**	A	*GW*	PM
42008	*	**FG**	A	*GW*	PM	42025	**FG**	A	*GW*	PM
42009		**FG**	A	*GW*	PM	42026	**FG**	A	*GW*	PM
42010		**FG**	A	*GW*	PM	42027	**FG**	A	*GW*	PM
42012	*	**FG**	A	*GW*	PM	42028	**FG**	A	*GW*	PM
42013		**FG**	A	*GW*	PM	42029	**FG**	A	*GW*	PM
42014		**FG**	A	*GW*	PM	42030	*	**FG**	A	*GW*	PM
42015	*	**FG**	A	*GW*	PM	42031	**FG**	A	*GW*	PM

No.					
42032		**FG**	A	*GW*	PM
42033		**FG**	A	*GW*	LA
42034		**FG**	A	*GW*	LA
42035		**FG**	A	*GW*	LA
42036	u	**MN**	A	*MM*	NL
42037	u	**MN**	A	*MM*	NL
42038	u	**MN**	A	*MM*	NL
42039		**FG**	A	*GW*	LA
42040		**FG**	A	*GW*	LA
42041		**FG**	A	*GW*	LA
42042		**FG**	A	*GW*	LA
42043		**FG**	A	*GW*	LA
42044		**FG**	A	*GW*	LA
42045		**FG**	A	*GW*	LA
42046		**FG**	A	*GW*	LA
42047		**FG**	A	*GW*	LA
42048		**FG**	A	*GW*	LA
42049		**FG**	A	*GW*	LA
42050		**FG**	A	*GW*	LA
42051	u	**MN**	A	*MM*	NL
42052	u	**MN**	A	*MM*	NL
42053	u	**MN**	A	*MM*	NL
42054		**FG**	A	*GW*	LA
42055		**FG**	A	*GW*	LA
42056		**FG**	A	*GW*	LA
42057		**GN**	A	*GN*	EC
42058		**GN**	A	*GN*	EC
42059		**GN**	A	*GN*	EC
42060		**FG**	A	*GW*	LA
42061		**FG**	A	*GW*	PM
42062	*	**FG**	A	*GW*	LA
42063		**GN**	A	*GN*	EC
42064		**GN**	A	*GN*	EC
42065		**GN**	A	*GN*	EC
42066	*	**FG**	A	*GW*	LA
42067		**FG**	A	*GW*	LA
42068		**FG**	A	*GW*	LA
42069	*	**FG**	A	*GW*	LA
42070		**FG**	A	*GW*	LA
42071		**FG**	A	*GW*	LA
42072		**FG**	A	*GW*	PM
42073		**FG**	A	*GW*	LA
42074		**FG**	A	*GW*	LA
42075		**FG**	A	*GW*	PM
42076	e	**0**	A	*GW*	LA
42077		**FG**	A	*GW*	LA
42078		**FG**	A	*GW*	LA
42079		**FG**	A	*GW*	PM
42080		**FG**	A	*GW*	PM
42081	*	**FG**	A	*GW*	LA
42083		**FG**	A	*GW*	LA
42084	s	**MN**	P	*VX*	NL
42085	t	**MN**	P	*VX*	NL
42086	s	**MN**	P	*VX*	NL
42087	s	**MN**	P	*VX*	NL
42088	s	**V**	P		BR
42089		**FG**	A	*GW*	PM
42090	s	**V**	P		BR
42091	†	**GN**	A	*GN*	EC
42092	s	**V**	FG		BR
42093	s	**V**	FG		BR
42094	s	**V**	FG		BR
42095	s	**V**	FG		LA
42096		**FG**	A	*GW*	LA
42097	w	**MN**	A	*MM*	NL
42098		**FG**	A	*GW*	PM
42099		**FG**	A	*GW*	LA
42100	u	**MN**	P	*MM*	NL
42101	w	**MN**	P	*MM*	NL
42102	u	**MN**	P	*MM*	NL
42103	z	**GN**	P	*GN*	EC
42104		**GN**	A	*GN*	EC
42105	s	**V**	FG		BR
42106		**GN**	A	*GN*	EC
42107		**FG**	A	*GW*	LA
42108	s	**V**	FG		BR
42109	s	**V**	P		BR
42110	s	**V**	P		BR
42111	u	**MN**	P	*MM*	NL
42112	u	**MN**	P	*MM*	NL
42113	u	**MN**	P	*MM*	NL
42115	t	**MN**	P	*VX*	NL
42116	†	**GN**	A	*GN*	EC
42117		**GN**	A	*GN*	EC
42118		**FG**	A	*GW*	LA
42119	u	**MN**	P	*MM*	NL
42120	u	**MN**	P	*MM*	NL
42121	u	**MN**	P	*MM*	NL
42122		**GN**	A	*GN*	EC
42123	u	**MN**	P	*MM*	NL
42124	u	**MN**	P	*MM*	NL
42125	u	**MN**	P	*MM*	NL
42126		**FG**	A	*GW*	LA
42127	†	**GN**	A	*GN*	EC
42128	†	**GN**	A	*GN*	EC
42129		**FG**	A	*GW*	LA
42130	t	**V**	P		BR
42131	u	**MN**	P	*MM*	NL
42132	u	**MN**	P	*MM*	NL
42133	u	**MN**	P	*MM*	NL
42134		**GN**	A	*GN*	EC
42135	u	**MN**	P	*MM*	NL

42136 u	MN	P	MM	NL
42137 u	MN	P	MM	NL
42138 *	FG	A	GW	PM
42139 ✔	MN	P	MM	NL
42140 u	MN	P	MM	NL
42141 ✔	MN	P	MM	NL
42143	FG	A	GW	LA
42144	FG	A	GW	LA
42145	FG	A	GW	LA
42146 ⁄	GN	A	GN	EC
42147 ✔u	MN	P	MM	NL
42148 u	MN	P	MM	NL
42149 u	MN	P	MM	NL
42150	GN	A	GN	EC
42151 w	MN	P	MM	NL
42152 u	MN	P	MM	NL
42153 u	MN	P	MM	NL
42154	GN	A	GN	EC
42155 w	MN	P	MM	NL
42156 u	MN	P	MM	NL
42157 u	MN	P	MM	NL
42158	GN	A	GN	EC
42159 s	V	P		BR
42160 s	V	P		BR
42161 †	GN	A	GN	EC
42162	FG	P	GW	LA
42163 w	MN	P	MM	NL
42164 u	MN	P	MM	NL
42165 u	MN	P	MM	NL
42166	FG	P	GW	LA
42167	GN	P	GN	EC
42168	GN	P	GN	EC
42169	GN	P	GN	EC
42170	FG	P	GW	LA
42171	GN	A	GN	EC
42172	GN	A	GN	EC
42173	FG	P	GW	LA
42174	FG	P	GW	LA
42175 s	V	FG		BR
42176 t	V	FG		BR
42177 s	V	FG		BR
42178 t	MN	P	VX	NL
42179	GN	A	GN	EC
42180	GN	A	GN	EC
42181	GN	A	GN	EC
42182	GN	A	GN	EC
42183 *	FG	A	GW	LA
42184	FG	A	GW	LA
42185	FG	A	GW	LA
42186	GN	A	GN	EC
42187 t	MN	P		BR
42188 †	GN	A	GN	EC
42189 †	GN	A	GN	EC
42190	GN	A	GN	EC
42191	GN	A	GN	EC
42192	GN	A	GN	EC
42193	GN	A	GN	EC
42194 w	MN	P	MM	NL
42195	FG	P	GW	LA
42196	FG	A	GW	LA
42197	FG	A	GW	LA
42198	GN	A	GN	EC
42199	GN	A	GN	EC
42200 *	FG	A	GW	LA
42201 *	FG	A	GW	LA
42202 *	FG	A	GW	LA
42203	FG	A	GW	LA
42204	FG	A	GW	LA
42205 u	MN	P	MM	NL
42206 *	FG	A	GW	LA
42207 *	FG	A	GW	LA
42208	FG	A	GW	LA
42209	FG	A	GW	LA
42210 u	MN	P	MM	NL
42211 *	FG	A	GW	PM
42212	FG	A	GW	PM
42213	FG	A	GW	PM
42214	FG	A	GW	PM
42215	GN	A	GN	EC
42216	FG	A	GW	LA
42217	FG	P	GW	LA
42218	FG	P	GW	LA
42219	GN	A	GN	EC
42220 w	MN	P	MM	NL
42221	FG	A	GW	LA
42222	FG	P	GW	LA
42223	FG	P	GW	LA
42224	FG	P	GW	LA
42225 u	MN	P	MM	NL
42226	GN	A	GN	EC
42227 u	MN	P	MM	NL
42228 u	MN	P	MM	NL
42229 u	MN	P	MM	NL
42230 u	MN	P	MM	NL
42231 s	V	FG		LA
42232 t	V	FG		LA
42233 s	V	FG		LA
42234 s	V	P		BR
42235	GN	A	GN	EC
42236	FG	A	GW	PM
42237 s	GN	P	GN	EC
42238 †	GN	A	GN	EC

No.					
42239 †	**GN**	A	*GN*	EC
42240	**GN**	A	*GN*	EC
42241	**GN**	A	*GN*	EC
42242	**GN**	A	*GN*	EC
42243	**GN**	A	*GN*	EC
42244	**GN**	A	*GN*	EC
42245	**FG**	A	*GW*	LA
42246 s	**MN**	P	*MM*	NL
42247 t	**MN**	P	*MM*	NL
42248 s	**MN**	P	*MM*	NL
42249 s	**MN**	P	*MM*	NL
42250	**FG**	A	*GW*	LA
42251 *	**FG**	A	*GW*	PM
42252	**FG**	A	*GW*	LA
42253	**FG**	A	*GW*	LA
42254	**FG**	P	*GW*	LA
42255 *	**FG**	A	*GW*	PM
42256	**FG**	A	*GW*	PM
42257	**FG**	A	*GW*	PM
42258	**FG**	P	*GW*	LA
42259 *	**FG**	A	*GW*	PM
42260	**FG**	A	*GW*	LA
42261	**FG**	A	*GW*	LA
42262	**FG**	P	*GW*	LA
42263	**FG**	A	*GW*	PM
42264 *	**FG**	A	*GW*	PM
42265	**FG**	A	*GW*	LA
42266	**FG**	P	*GW*	LA
42267 *	**FG**	A	*GW*	PM
42268 *	**FG**	A	*GW*	LA
42269	**FG**	A	*GW*	PM
42271 *	**FG**	A	*GW*	LA
42272	**FG**	A	*GW*	LA
42273	**FG**	A	*GW*	LA
42275 *	**FG**	A	*GW*	LA
42276	**FG**	A	*GW*	LA
42277	**FG**	A	*GW*	LA
42279 *	**FG**	A	*GW*	LA
42280	**FG**	A	*GW*	LA
42281	**FG**	A	*GW*	LA
42283	**FG**	A	*GW*	LA
42284	**FG**	A	*GW*	PM
42285	**FG**	A	*GW*	PM
42286 s	**V**	P		BR
42287 *	**FG**	A	*GW*	LA
42288	**FG**	A	*GW*	LA
42289	**FG**	A	*GW*	LA
42290 t	**V**	P		BR
42291 *	**FG**	A	*GW*	LA
42292 *	**FG**	A	*GW*	LA
42293	**FG**	A	*GW*	LA
42294 s	**V**	P		BR
42295 *	**FG**	A	*GW*	LA
42296	**FG**	A	*GW*	LA
42297	**FG**	A	*GW*	LA
42299 *	**FG**	A	*GW*	LA
42300	**FG**	A	*GW*	LA
42301	**FG**	A	*GW*	LA
42302 s	**V**	FG		WS
42303 t	**V**	FG		WS
42304 s	**V**	FG		WS
42305 s	**V**	FG		WS
42306 s	**GN**	P	*GN*	EC
42307 s	**GN**	P	*GN*	EC
42308 s	**MN**	P	*VX*	NL
42309 s	**MN**	P	*VX*	NL
42314	**FG**	P	*GW*	LA
42315	**FG**	P	*GW*	LA
42316	**FG**	P	*GW*	LA
42317	**FG**	P	*GW*	LA
42318 s	**V**	P		NL
42319 t	**V**	P		NL
42320 s	**V**	P		BR
42321 s	**V**	P		BR
42322 s	**V**	P		BR
42323	**GN**	A	*GN*	EC
42324 w	**MN**	P	*MM*	NL
42325	**FG**	A	*GW*	LA
42326 s	**GN**	A	*GN*	EC
42327 w	**MN**	P	*MM*	NL
42328 w	**MN**	P	*MM*	NL
42329 w	**MN**	P	*MM*	NL
42330 s	**GN**	P	*GN*	EC
42331 w	**MN**	P	*MM*	NL
42332	**FG**	A	*GW*	PM
42333	**FG**	A	*GW*	LA
42334	**FG**	P	*GW*	LA
42335 u	**MN**	P	*MM*	NL
42336 s	**MN**	P	*VX*	NL
42337 w	**MN**	P	*MM*	NL
42338 s	**MN**	P	*VX*	NL
42339 w	**MN**	P	*MM*	NL
42340	**GN**	A	*GN*	EC
42341 u	**MN**	P	*MM*	NL

No.						
42342 (44082)	u	**MN**	A	*MM*	NL
42343 (44095)		**FG**	A	*GW*	LA
42344 (44092)	*	**FG**	A	*GW*	LA

42345	(44096)	*	**FG**	A	*GW*	LA
42346	(41053)		**FG**	A	*GW*	PM
42347	(41054)	*	**FG**	A	*GW*	LA
42348	(41073)	*	**FG**	A	*GW*	LA
42349	(41074)		**FG**	A	*GW*	PM
42350	(41047)		**FG**	A	*GW*	LA
42351	(41048)		**FG**	A	*GW*	LA
42352	(42142, 41176)	u	**MN**	P	*MM*	NL
42353	(42001, 41171)	§	**O**	FG		SW
42354	(42114, 41175)		**GN**	A	*GN*	EC
42355	(42000, 41172)		**GN**	A	*GN*	EC
42356	(42002, 41173)		**FG**	A	*GW*	PM
42357	(41002, 41174)		**GN**	A	*GN*	EC
42360	(44084, 45084)		**FG**	A	*GW*	PM
42361	(44099, 42000)		**FG**	A	*GW*	LA
42362	(42011, 41178)		**FG**	A	*GW*	LA
42363	(41082)	†	**GN**	A	*GN*	EC

GJ2G (TGS)   TRAILER GUARD'S STANDARD

44000. Lot No. 30953 Derby 1980. 33.47 t.
44001–44090. Lot No. 30949 Derby 1980–82. 33.47 t.
44091–44094. Lot No. 30964 Derby 1982. 33.47 t.
44097–44101. Lot No. 30970 Derby 1982. 33.47 t.

As built –/65 1T (w –/63 1T 1W). pg.
st Fitted with centre luggage stack s –/63 1T, t –/61 1T.

44000	w	**FG**	P	*GW*	LA	44025	w	**FG**	A	*GW*	LA
44001	w	**FG**	A	*GW*	LA	44026	w	**FG**	A	*GW*	PM
44002	w	**FG**	A	*GW*	PM	44027	s	**MN**	P	*MM*	NL
44003	w	**FG**	A	*GW*	PM	44028	w	**FG**	A	*GW*	LA
44004	w	**FG**	A	*GW*	PM	44029	w	**FG**	A	*GW*	PM
44005	w	**FG**	A	*GW*	PM	44030	w	**FG**	A	*GW*	LA
44007	w	**FG**	A	*GW*	PM	44031	w	**GN**	A	*GN*	EC
44008	w	**FG**	A	*GW*	PM	44032	w	**FG**	A	*GW*	PM
44009	w	**FG**	A	*GW*	PM	44033	w	**FG**	A	*GW*	LA
44010	w	**FG**	A	*GW*	PM	44034	w	**FG**	A	*GW*	LA
44011	w	**FG**	A	*GW*	LA	44035	w	**FG**	A	*GW*	LA
44012	s	**MN**	A	*MM*	NL	44036	w	**FG**	A	*GW*	PM
44013	w	**FG**	A	*GW*	LA	44037	w	**FG**	A	*GW*	LA
44014	w	**FG**	A	*GW*	LA	44038	w	**FG**	A	*GW*	LA
44015	w	**FG**	A	*GW*	LA	44039	w	**FG**	A	*GW*	LA
44016	w	**FG**	A	*GW*	LA	44040	w	**FG**	A	*GW*	LA
44017	s	**MN**	A	*MM*	NL	44041	s	**MN**	P	*MM*	NL
44018	w	**FG**	A	*GW*	LA	44042	t	**MN**	P	*VX*	NL
44019	w	**GN**	A	*GN*	EC	44043	w	**FG**	A	*GW*	LA
44020	w	**FG**	A	*GW*	LA	44044	s	**MN**	P	*MM*	NL
44021	t	**V**	P		BR	44045	w	**GN**	A	*GN*	EC
44022	w	**FG**	A	*GW*	LA	44046	s	**MN**	P	*MM*	NL
44023	w	**FG**	A	*GW*	LA	44047	s	**MN**	P	*MM*	NL
44024	w	**FG**	A	*GW*	LA	44048	s	**MN**	P	*MM*	NL

44049	w	**FG**	A	*GW*	LA	44073	s	**MN**	P	*MM*	NL
44050	s	**MN**	P	*MM*	NL	44074	t	**V**	FG		LA
44051	s	**MN**	P	*MM*	NL	44075	t	**GN**	P	*GN*	EC
44052	s	**MN**	P	*MM*	NL	44076	t	**V**	FG		BR
44054	w	**MN**	P	*MM*	NL	44077	w	**GN**	A	*GN*	EC
44055	w	**GN**	P	*GN*	EC	44078	t	**MN**	P	*MM*	NL
44056	w	**GN**	A	*GN*	EC	44079	w	**FG**	P	*GW*	LA
44057	t	**V**	P		BR	44080	w	**GN**	A	*GN*	EC
44058	w	**GN**	A	*GN*	EC	44081	t	**V**	FG		BR
44059	w	**FG**	A	*GW*	LA	44083	s	**MN**	P	*MM*	NL
44060	t	**MN**	P	*VX*	NL	44085	s	**MN**	P	*MM*	NL
44061	w	**GN**	A	*GN*	EC	44086	w	**FG**	A	*GW*	LA
44062	t	**MN**	P	*VX*	NL	44088	t	**V**	P		BR
44063	w	**GN**	A	*GN*	EC	44089	t	**V**	P		BR
44064	w	**FG**	A	*GW*	LA	44090	w	**FG**	P	*GW*	LA
44065	t	**V**	P		BR	44091	t	**V**	P		BR
44066	w	**FG**	A	*GW*	LA	44093	w	**FG**	A	*GW*	LA
44067	w	**FG**	A	*GW*	PM	44094	w	**GN**	A	*GN*	EC
44068	t	**V**	FG		WS	44097	w	**FG**	P	*GW*	LA
44069	t	**MN**	P	*VX*	NL	44098	w	**GN**	A	*GN*	EC
44070	s	**MN**	P	*MM*	NL	44100	t	**V**	FG		OO
44071	s	**MN**	P	*MM*	NL	44101	w	**FG**	P	*GW*	LA
44072	t	**V**	P		BR						

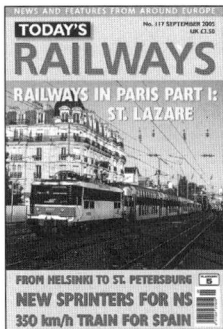

3. SALOONS

Several specialist passenger carrying vehicles, normally referred to as saloons are permitted to run on the National Rail system. Many of these are to pre-nationalisation designs.

WCJS FIRST SALOON

Built 1892 by LNWR, Wolverton. Originally dining saloon mounted on six-wheel bogies. Rebuilt with new underframe with four-wheel bogies in 1927. Rebuilt 1960 as observation saloon with DMU end. Gangwayed at other end. The interior has a saloon, kitchen, guards vestibule and observation lounge. Gresley bogies. 19/– 1T. 28.5 t. 75 m.p.h.

Non-Standard Livery: London & North Western Railway.

41   (484, 45018)   x   **0**   SH   *SH*   CJ

LNWR DINING SALOON

Built 1890 by LNWR, Wolverton. Mounted on the underframe of LMS GUV 37908 in the 1980s. Contains kitchen and dining area seating 12 at tables for two. Gresley bogies. 10/–. 75 m.p.h. 25.4 t.

Non-Standard Livery: London & North Western Railway.

159   (5159)   x   **0**   SH   *SH*   CJ

GNR FIRST CLASS SALOON

Built 1912 by GNR, Doncaster. Contains entrance vestibule, lavatory, two seperate saloons, library and luggage space. Gresley bogies. 19/– 1T. 75 m.p.h. 29.4 t.

Non-Standard Livery: Teak.

807   (4807)   x   **0**   SH   *SH*   CJ

LNER GENERAL MANAGERS SALOON

Built 1945 by LNER, York. Gangwayed at one end with a verandah at the other. The interior has a dining saloon seating twelve, kitchen, toilet, office and nine seat lounge. 21/– 1T. B4 bogies. 75 m.p.h. ETH3. 35.7 t.

1999   (902260)   **M**   GS   *GS*   CS   DINING CAR No. 2

GENERAL MANAGER'S SALOON

Renumbered 1989 from London Midland Region departmental series. Formerly the LMR General Manager's saloon. Rebuilt from LMS period 1 BFK M 5033 M to dia. 1654 and mounted on the underframe of BR suburban BS M 43232. Screw couplings have been removed. B4 bogies. 100 m.p.h. ETH2X.

LMS Lot No. 326 Derby 1927. 27.5 t.

6320   (5033, DM 395707) x   **M**   62   *62*   SK

GWR FIRST CLASS SALOON

Built 1930 by GWR, Swindon. Contains saloons at either end with body end observation windows, staff compartment, central kitchen and pantry/bar. Numbered DE321011 when in departmental service with British Railways. 20/– 1T. GWR bogies. 75 m.p.h. 34 t.

GWR Lot No. 1431 1930.

9004   **CH**   RA   *SH*   CJ

LMS INSPECTION SALOONS

Built as engineers inspection saloons. Non-gangwayed. Observation windows at each end. The interior layout consists of two saloons interspersed by a central lavatory/kitchen/guards section. BR Mark 1 bogies. 80 m.p.h. 31.5 t.

45020–45026. Lot No. LMS 1356 Wolverton 1944.
45029. Lot No. LMS 1327 Wolverton 1942.
999503. Lot No. BR Wagon Lot. 3093 Wolverton 1957.

45020		**E**	E	*E*	ML
45026	v	**M**	HN		CS
45029	v	**E**	E		ML
999503	v	**M**	E		OM

"QUEEN OF SCOTS" SERVICE CARS

Converted from BR Mark 1 BSKs. Commonwealth bogies. 100 m.p.h. ETH2.

Non-Standard Livery: London & North Western Railway.

99035. Lot No. 30699 Wolverton 1962–63.
99886. Lot No. 30721 Wolverton 1963.

99035 (35322)	x	**0**	SH	*SH*	CJ	SERVICE CAR No. 2
99886 (35407)	x	**0**	SH	*SH*	CJ	SERVICE CAR No. 1

VSOE SUPPORT CARS

Converted 1983 (§ 199x) from BR Nark 1 BSK (§Courier vehicle converted from Mark 1 BSK 1986–87). Toilet retained and former compartment area replaced with train manager's office, crew locker room, linen store and dry goods store. The former luggage area has been adapted for use as an engineers' compartment and workshop. Commonwealth bogies. 100 m.p.h. ETH2.

99538. Lot No. 30229 Metro-Cammell 1955–57. 36 t.
99545. Lot No. 30721 Wolverton 1963. 37 t.

99538 (34991)		**PC**	VS	*VS*	SL	BAGGAGE CAR No. 9
99545 (35466, 80207) §	**PC**	VS	*VS*	SL	BAGGAGE CAR No. 11

RAILFILMS KITCHEN/SLEEPING SALOON

Converted from BR Mark 1 SK. Contains three sleeping cabins with showers and toilets and a large kitchen/pantry. Commonwealth bogies. 100 m.p.h. ETH 4.

Lot No. 30726 York 1963.

Non-standard Livery: London & North Western Railway.

99884 (26208, 19208) **0**	RA		CS	State Car No. 84

ROYAL SCOTSMAN SALOONS

Built 1960 by Metro-Cammell as Pullman Parlour First (§Pullman Kitchen First) for East Coast Main Line services. Rebuilt 1990 as sleeping cars with four twin sleeping rooms (*§ three twin sleeping rooms and two single sleeping rooms at each end). Commonwealth bogies. 38.5 t.

99961 (324 AMBER) *	**M**	GS	*GS*	CS	STATE CAR 1
99962 (329 PEARL)	**M**	GS	*GS*	CS	STATE CAR 2
99963 (331 TOPAZ)	**M**	GS	*GS*	CS	STATE CAR 3
99964 (313 FINCH) §	**M**	GS	*GS*	CS	STATE CAR 4

Built 1960 by Metro-Cammell as Pullman Kitchen First for East Coast Main Line services. Rebuilt 1990 as observation car with open verandah seating 32. Commonwealth bogies. 38.5 t.

99965 (319 SNIPE)	**M**	GS	*GS*	CS	OBSERVATION CAR

Built 1960 by Metro-Cammell as Pullman Kitchen First for East Coast Main Line services. Rebuilt 1993 as dining car. Commonwealth bogies. 38.5 t.

99967 (317 RAVEN)	**M**	GS	*GS*	CS	DINING CAR

Mark 3A. Converted from SLEP at Carnforth Railway Restoration and Engineering Services in 1997. BT10 bogies. Attendant's and adjacent two sleeping compartments converted to generator room containing a 160 kW Volvo unit. In 99968 four sleeping compartments remain for staff use with another converted for use as a staff shower and toilet. The remaining five sleeping compartments have been replaced by two passenger cabins. In 99969 seven sleeping compartments remain for staff use. A further sleeping compartment, along with one toilet, have been converted to store rooms. The other two sleeping compartments have been combined to form a crew mess. ETH7X. 41.5 t.

Lot. No. 30960 Derby 1981–3.

99968 (10541)	**M**	GS	*GS*	CS	STATE CAR 5
99969 (10556)	**M**	GS	*GS*	CS	SERVICE CAR

RAILFILMS 'LMS CLUB CAR'

Converted from BR Mark 1 TSO at Carnforth Railway Restoration and Engineering Services in 1994. Contains kitchenette, pantry, coupé, lounge/reception area with two settees and two dining saloons. 24/– 1T. Commonwealth bogies. 100 m.p.h. ETH 4.

Lot. No. 30724 York 1963. 37 t.

99993 (5067)	**M**	RA	*WT*	OM	LMS CLUB CAR

BR INSPECTION SALOON

Mark 1. Short frames. Non-gangwayed. Observation windows at each end. The interior layout consists of two saloons interspersed by a central lavatory/kitchen/guards/luggage section. BR Mark 1 bogies. 90 m.p.h.

Lot No. BR Wagon Lot. 3379 Swindon 1960. 30.5 t.

999509	**E**	E	*E*	ML

4. PULLMAN CAR COMPANY SERIES

Pullman cars have never generally been numbered as such, although many have carried numbers, instead they have carried titles. However, a scheme of schedule numbers exists which generally lists cars in chronological order. In this section those numbers are shown followed by the car's title. Cars described as 'kitchen' contain a kitchen in addition to passenger accommodation and have gas cooking unless otherwise stated. Cars described as 'parlour' consist entirely of passenger accomodation. Cars described as 'brake' contain a compartment for the use of the guard and a luggage compartment in addition to passenger accommodation.

PULLMAN PARLOUR FIRST

Built 1927 by Midland Carriage and Wagon Company. Gresley bogies. 26/– 2T. ETH 2. 41 t.

213 MINERVA   **PC** VS *VS* SL

PULLMAN PARLOUR FIRST

Built 1928 by Metropolitan Carriage and Wagon Company. Gresley bogies. 24/– 2T. ETH 4. 40 t.

239 AGATHA   **PC** VS   SL
243 LUCILLE   **PC** VS *VS*   SL

PULLMAN KITCHEN FIRST

Built 1925 by BRCW. Rebuilt by Midland Carriage & Wagon Company in 1928. Gresley bogies. 20/– 1T. ETH 4. 41 t.

245 IBIS   **PC** VS *VS* SL

PULLMAN PARLOUR FIRST

Built 1928 by Metropolitan Carriage and Wagon Company. Gresley bogies. 24/– 2T. ETH 4.

254 ZENA   **PC** VS *VS* SL

PULLMAN KITCHEN FIRST

Built 1928 by Metropolitan Carriage and Wagon Company. Gresley bogies. 20/– 1T. ETH 4. 42 t.

255 IONE   **PC** VS *VS* SL

PULLMAN KITCHEN COMPOSITE

Built 1932 by Metropolitan Carriage and Wagon Company. Originally included in 6-Pul EMU. Electric cooking. EMU bogies. 12/16 1T.

264	RUTH	**PC**	VS		SL

PULLMAN KITCHEN FIRST

Built 1932 by Metopolitan Carriage and Wagon Company. Originally included in 'Brighton Belle' EMUs but now used as hauled stock. Electric cooking. B5 (SR) bogies (§ EMU bogies). 20/– 1T. ETH 2. 44 t.

280	AUDREY		**PC**	VS		SL
281	GWEN		**PC**	VS	*VS*	SL
283	MONA	§	**PC**	VS		SL
284	VERA		**PC**	VS	*VS*	SL

PULLMAN PARLOUR THIRD

Built 1932 by Metropolitan Carriage and Wagon Company. Originally included in 'Brighton Belle' EMUs. EMU bogies. –/56 2T.

285	CAR No. 85	**PC**	VS		SL
286	CAR No. 86	**PC**	VS		SL

PULLMAN BRAKE THIRD

Built 1932 by Metropolitan Carriage and Wagon Company. Originally driving motor cars in 'Brighton Belle' EMUs. Traction and control equipment removed for use as hauled stock. EMU bogies. –/48 1T.

288	CAR No. 88	**PC**	VS		SL
292	CAR No. 92	**PC**	VS		SL
293	CAR No. 93	**PC**	VS		SL

PULLMAN PARLOUR FIRST

Built 1951 by Birmingham Railway Carriage and Wagon Company. Gresley bogies. 32/– 2T. ETH 3. 39 t.

301	PERSEUS	**PC**	VS	*VS*	SL

Built 1952 by Pullman Car Company, Preston Park using underframe and bogies from 176 RAINBOW, the body of which had been destroyed by fire. Gresley bogies. 26/– 2T. ETH 4. 38 t.

302	PHOENIX	**PC**	VS	*VS*	SL

PULLMAN PARLOUR FIRST

Built 1951 by Birmingham Railway Carriage & Wagon Company. Gresley bogies. 32/– 2T. ETH 3. 39 t.

308 CYGNUS   **PC** VS   *VS*   SL

PULLMAN FIRST BAR

Built 1951 by Birmingham Railway Carriage & Wagon Company. Rebuilt 1999 by Blake Fabrications, Edinburgh with original timber-framed body replaced by a new fabricated steel body. Contains kitchen, bar, dining saloon and coupé. Electric cooking. Gresley bogies. 14/– 1T. ETH 3.

310 PEGASUS   **PC** RA   *WT*   OM

Also carries "THE TRIANON BAR" branding.

PULLMAN KITCHEN SECOND

Built 1960–1961 by Metro-Cammell for East Coast Main Line services. Commonwealth bogies. –/30 1T. 40 t.

335 CAR No. 335   x   **PC** VT   *VT*   TM

PULLMAN PARLOUR SECOND

Built 1960–1961 by Metro-Cammell for East Coast Main Line services. Commonwealth bogies. –/42 2T. 38.5 t.

348 CAR No. 348   x   **PC** WC   CS
353 CAR No. 353   x   **PC** VT   *VT*   TM

PULLMAN SECOND BAR

Built 1960–1961 by Metro-Cammell for East Coast Main Line services. Commonwealth bogies. –/24 + 17 bar seats. 38.5 t.

354 CAR No. 354   x   **PC** WC   CS

Formerly also known as "THE HADRIAN BAR".

5. PASSENGER COACHING STOCK AWAITING DISPOSAL

This list contains the last known locations of coaching stock awaiting disposal. The definition of which vehicles are "awaiting disposal" is somewhat vague, but generally speaking these are vehicles of types not now in normal service or vehicles which have been damaged by fire, vandalism or collision.

1644 CS	5443 KT	10604 OM
1650 CS	5446 KT	10646 TO
1652 CS	5454 KT	10653 OM
1653 FP	5471 KT	10654 OM
1655 CS	5475 KT	10664 ZN
1663 CS	5480 KT	10669 OM
1670 CS	5505 CS	10677 ZN
1674 SL	5616 FP	10682 OM
1688 CS	5781 NC	10686 OM
1981 OM	6178 HM	10695 ZN
2127 CS	6335 LA	10709 ZN
3225 KT	6339 EC	10711 OM
3226 KT	6345 EC	10712 OM
3246 CS	6356 BH	10713 OM
3258 KT	6357 BH	10721 ZN
4849 CD	6360 NL	10730 OM
4854 CD	6361 NL	13306 CS
4860 CS	6523 CS	13320 CS
4932 CS	6900 Cambridge Station Yard	13323 CS
4997 CS	6901 Cambridge Station Yard	13582 KT
5042 FP	9385 LT	13604 FP
5226 LT	9458 ZB	13607 FP
5265 KT	9482 NL	17058 KT
5267 KT	10327 ZC	18837 CS
5354 PY	10533 MM	19013 CS
5389 OM	10540 OM	34525 CS
5410 KT	10554 OM	35509 ZH
5420 OM	10572 OM	35513 CD
5433 TM	10574 TO	35516 KT

6. 99xxx RANGE NUMBER CONVERSION TABLE

The following table is presented to help readers identify vehicles which may carry numbers in the 99xxx range, the former private owner number series which is no longer in general use.

99xxx	BR No.	99xxx	BR No.	99xxx	BR No.	99xxx	BR No.
99040	21232	99322	5600	99534	Pullman 245	99678	504
99041	35476	99323	5704	99535	Pullman 213	99679	506
99052	Saloon 41	99324	5714	99536	Pullman 254	99680	17102
99121	3105	99325	5727	99537	Pullman 280	99710	18767
99125	3113	99326	4954	99539	Pullman 255	99712	18893
99127	3117	99327	5044	99541	Pullman 243	99716	18808
99128	3130	99328	5033	99542	889202	99718	18862
99131	1999	99329	4931	99543	Pullman 284	99721	18756
99141	17041	99348	Pullman 348	99546	Pullman 281	99722	18806
99304	21256	99353	Pullman 353	99670	546	99723	35459
99311	1882	99354	Pullman 354	99671	548	99792	17019
99312	35463	99361	Pullman 335	99672	549	99880	159
99316	13321	99371	3128	99673	550	99881	807
99317	3766	99405	35486	99674	551	99953	35468
99318	4912	99530	Pullman 301	99675	552		
99319	17168	99531	Pullman 302	99676	553		
99321	5299	99532	Pullman 308	99677	586		

7. PRESERVED LOCOMOTIVE SUPPORT COACHES TABLE

The following table lists support coaches and the BR numbers of the locomotives which they normally support at present. These coaches can spend considerable periods of time off the National Rail system when the locomotives they support are not being used on that system.

14007	61264	35317	34067	35465	46035	35508	BQ locos
17013	60019	35329	RL locos	35468	NM locos	35517	BQ locos
17019	46201	35333	6024	35470	TM locos	35518	34067
17041	71000	35453	5051	35476	46233	80204	WC locos
17096	35028	35461	5029	35479	SV locos	80217	WC locos
21232	46233	35463	WC locos	35486	SV locos	80220	62005

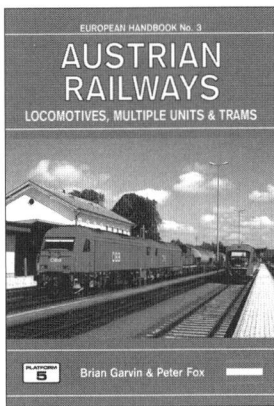

8. NON-PASSENGER-CARRYING COACHING STOCK

The notes shown for locomotive-hauled passenger stock generally apply also to non-passenger-carrying coaching stock (often abbreviated to NPCCS).

TOPS TYPE CODES

TOPS type codes for NPCCS are made up as follows:

(1) Two letters denoting the type of the vehicle:

AX	Nightstar generator van
AY	Eurostar barrier vehicle
NA	Propelling control vehicle.
NB	High security brake van (100 m.p.h.).
ND	Gangwayed brake van (90 m.p.h.).
NE	Gangwayed brake van (100 m.p.h.).
NH	Gangwayed brake van (110 m.p.h.).
NI	High security brake van (110 m.p.h.).
NJ	General utility van (90 m.p.h.).
NK	High security general utility van (100 m.p.h.).
NL	Newspaper van.
NN	Courier vehicle.
NO	General utility van (100 m.p.h. e.t.h. wired).
NP	Motorail van (110 m.p.h.).
NQ	High security brake van (110 m.p.h.).
NR	BAA container van (100 m.p.h.).
NV	Motorail van (side loading).
NX	Motorail van (110 m.p.h.).
NY	Exhibition van.
NZ	Driving brake van (also known as driving van trailer).
YR	Ferry van (special Southern Region version of NJ with two pairs of side doors instead of three).

(2) A third letter denoting the brake type:

A	Air braked
V	Vacuum braked
X	Dual braked

OPERATING CODES

The normal operating codes are given in parentheses after the TOPS type codes. These are as follows:

BG	Gangwayed brake van.
BV	Barrier vehicle.
DLV	Driving brake van (also known as driving van trailer – DVT).
GUV	General utility van.
PCV	Propelling control van.

AK51 (RK)   KITCHEN CAR

Mark 1. Converted 1989 from RBR. Fluorescent lighting. Commonwealth bogies. ETH 2X.

Lot No. 30628 Pressed Steel 1960–61. x. 39 t.

Note: Kitchen cars have traditionally been numbered in the NPCCS series, but have passenger coach diagram numbers!

80041   (1690)   **M**   E   *E*   OM

NN   COURIER VEHICLE

Mark 1. Converted 1986–7 from BSKs. One compartment and toilet retained for courier use. One set of roller shutter doors inserted on each side. x. ETH 2.

80204/17/23. Lot No. 30699 Wolverton 1962. Commonwealth bogies. 37 t.
80220. Lot No. 30573 Gloucester 1960. B4 bogies. 33 t.

Note: 80223 has been converted to a bar car with the former stowage area becoming an open saloon with a bar.

80204	(35297)	**M**	WC *LS*	CS
80217	(35299)	**M**	WC *LS*	CS
80220	(35276)	**M**	NE *LS*	NY
80223	(35331)	**G**	MH *MH*	RL

ND (BG) GANGWAYED BRAKE VAN (90 m.p.h.)

Mark 1. Short frames (57'). Load 10t. All vehicles were built with BR Mark 1 bogies. ETH 1. Vehicles numbered 81xxx had 3000 added to the original numbers to avoid confusion with Class 81 locomotives. The full lot number list is listed here for reference purposes with renumbered vehicles. No unmodified vehicles remain in service.

80621. Lot No. 30046 York 1954. 31.5 t.
80826. Lot No. 30144 Cravens 1955. 31.5 t.
80855–80959. Lot No. 30162 Pressed Steel 1956–57. 32 t.
80980–81001. Lot No. 30173 York 1956. 31.5 t.
81025–81026. Lot No. 30224 Cravens 1956. 31.5 t.
81077–81173. Lot No. 30228 Metro-Cammell 1957–58. 31.5 t.
81205–81265. Lot No. 30163 Pressed Steel 1957. 31.5 t.
81266–81309. Lot No. 30323 Pressed Steel 1957. 32 t.
81325–81497. Lot No. 30400 Pressed Steel 1957–58. 32 t.
81500–81568. Lot No. 30484 Pressed Steel 1958. 32 t.
81606. Lot No. 30716 Gloucester 1962. 31 t.

Non-standard Livery: 81025 is British racing green with gold lining.

The following vehicle is an ND rebogied with Commonwealth bogies and adapted for use as exhibition van 1998 at Lancastrian Carriage & Wagon Co. Ltd. 33 t.

81025   (81025, 84025)   **0**   RA   *RA*   CP
Name: 81025 VALIANT

NZ (DLV)   DRIVING BRAKE VAN (110 m.p.h.)

Mark 3B. Air conditioned. T4 bogies. dg. ETH 5X.

Lot No. 31042 Derby 1988. 45.18 t.

Non-standard Livery: 82146 is EWS silver.

82101	V	P	E	WB	82127	V	P	1A	NC
82102	1	P		ZB	82128	V	P	E	OM
82103	V	P		LT	82129	V	P		LT
82104	V	P	1A	NC	82130	V	P		LT
82105	V	P		WB	82131	V	P	E	OM
82106	V	P	SR	PC	82132	V	P	SR	PC
82107	V	P		PC	82133	V	P	1A	NC
82108	V	P		LT	82134	V	P		LT
82109	V	P		PC	82135	V	P		LT
82110	V	P		LT	82136	V	P	1A	NC
82111	V	P		LT	82137	V	P		LT
82112	V	P	SR	PC	82138	V	P		LT
82113	V	P		LT	82139	V	P		LT
82114	V	P	1A	NC	82140	V	P		LT
82115	V	P		LT	82141	V	P		LT
82116	V	P		LT	82142	V	P		LT
82117	V	P		LT	82143	V	P		LT
82118	V	P		WB	82144	V	P		LT
82119	1	P		CT	82145	V	P	E	OM
82120	V	P		PC	82146	0	E	E	TO
82121	V	P		LT	82147	V	P		LT
82122	V	P		LT	82148	V	P		LT
82123	V	P		LT	82149	V	P		LT
82124	V	P		LT	82150	V	P		LT
82125	V	P		WB	82151	V	P	E	OM
82126	V	P	E	WB	82152	V	P	1A	NC

Names:

82101   101 Squadron
82126   Wembley Traincare Centre

NZ (DLV)   DRIVING BRAKE VAN (140 m.p.h.)

Mark 4. Air conditioned. Swiss-built (SIG) bogies. dg. ETH 6X.

† Fitted with transceiver for wi-fi.

Lot No. 31043 Metro-Cammell 1988. 45.18 t.

82200		GN	H	GN	BN	82206		GN	H	GN	BN
82201		GN	H	GN	BN	82207		GN	H	GN	BN
82202		GN	H	GN	BN	82208	†	GN	H	GN	BN
82203		GN	H	GN	BN	82209	†	GN	H	GN	BN
82204	†	GN	H	GN	BN	82210		GN	H	GN	BN
82205	†	GN	H	GN	BN	82211	†	GN	H	GN	BN

82212	†	**GN**	H	*GN*	BN
82213	†	**GN**	H	*GN*	BN
82214	†	**GN**	H	*GN*	BN
82215	†	**GN**	H	*GN*	BN
82216		**GN**	H	*GN*	BN
82217		**GN**	H	*GN*	BN
82218	†	**GN**	H	*GN*	BN
82219	†	**GN**	H	*GN*	BN
82220		**GN**	H	*GN*	BN
82222		**GN**	H	*GN*	BN

82223	**GN**	H	*GN*	BN
82224	**GN**	H	*GN*	BN
82225	**GN**	H	*GN*	BN
82226	**GN**	H	*GN*	BN
82227	**GN**	H	*GN*	BN
82228	**GN**	H	*GN*	BN
82229	**GN**	H	*GN*	BN
82230	**GN**	H	*GN*	BN
82231	**GN**	H	*GN*	BN

Name:

82219   Duke of Edinburgh

NJ (GUV)   GENERAL UTILITY VAN

Mark 1. Short frames. Load 14 t. Screw couplings. These vehicles had 7000 added to the original numbers to avoid confusion with Class 86 locomotives. The full lot number list is listed here for reference purposes with renumbered vehicles. No unmodified vehicles remain in service. All vehicles were built with BR Mark 2 bogies. ETH 0 or 0X*.

86081–86499. Lot No. 30417 Pressed Steel 1958–59. 30 t.
86508–86518. Lot No. 30343 York 1957. 30 t.
86521–86648. Lot No. 30403 York/Glasgow 1958–60. 30 t.
86656–86820. Lot No. 30565 Pressed Steel 1959. 30 t.
86849–86956. Lot No. 30616 Pressed Steel 1959–60. 30 t.

NE/NH (BG) GANGWAYED BRAKE VAN (100/110 m.p.h.)

NE are ND but rebogied with B4 bogies suitable for 100 m.p.h. NH are identical but are allowed to run at 110 m.p.h. with special maintenance of the bogies. For lot numbers refer to original number series. Deduct 1.5t from weights. 92901–92938 were renumbered from 920xx series by adding 900 to number to avoid conflict with Class 92 locos. All NHA are *pg. ETH 1 (1X*).

92100	(81391)				RV	*VW*	CP
92111	(81432)		to		LW		CP
92125	(81470)		to		DR		KM
92159	(81534)		NHA		H		KT
92174	(81567)		NHA		H		PY
92175	(81568)		pg		H		CD
92194	(81606)		to		H		PY
92901	(80855, 92001)	NHA			H	*VW*	WB
92904	(80867, 92004)	*pg	G		VS		SL
92908	(80895, 92008)	NHA			WC		CS
92929	(81077, 92029)	NHA			LW		CP
92931	(81102, 92031)	NHA			H		PY
92935	(81150, 92035)	*pg			H		PY
92936	(81158, 92036)	NHA			H		CD
92938	(81173, 92038)	NHA			H		PY

NL   NEWSPAPER VAN

Mark 1. Short frames (57'). Converted from NJ (GUV). Fluorescent lighting, toilets and gangways fitted. Load 14 t. Now used for materials storage. B5 Bogies. ETH 3X.

Lot No. 30922 Wolverton 1977–78. 31 t.

94003	(86281, 93999)	x	**RX**	FG	*GW*	OO
94006	(86202, 85506)		**RX**	FG	*GW*	OO

NKA   HIGH SECURITY GENERAL UTILITY VAN

Mark 1. These vehicles are GUVs further modified with new floors, three roller shutter doors per side and the end doors removed. For lot Nos. see original number series. Commonwealth bogies. Add 2 t to weight. ETH0X.

Non-Standard Livery: 94121 is grey.

94100	(86668, 95100)	**RX**	E	ML
94101	(86142, 95101)	**RX**	E	TE
94102	(86762, 95102)	**RX**	E	OM
94103	(86956, 95103)	**RX**	E	SD
94104	(86942, 95104)	**RX**	E	OM
94106	(86353, 95106)	**RX**	E	*E*	ML
94107	(86576, 95107)	**RX**	E	OM
94108	(86600, 95108)	**RX**	E	OM
94110	(86393, 95110)	**RX**	E	ER
94111	(86578, 95111)	**RX**	E	ML
94112	(86673, 95112)	**RX**	E	OM
94113	(86235, 95113)	**RX**	E	OM
94114	(86081, 95114)	**RX**	E	WE
94116	(86426, 95116)	**RX**	E	TY
94117	(86534, 95117)	**RX**	E	TE
94118	(86675, 95118)	**RX**	E	EN
94119	(86167, 95119)	**RX**	E	TY
94121	(86518, 95121)	**0**	E	TO
94123	(86376, 95123)	**RX**	E	ML
94126	(86692, 95126)	**RX**	E	ER
94132	(86607, 95132)	**RX**	E	ML
94133	(86604, 95133)	**RX**	E	ML
94137	(86610, 95137)	**RX**	E	*E*	ML
94138	(86212, 95138)	**RX**	E	YN
94140	(86571, 95140)	**RX**	E	TY
94146	(86648, 95146)	**RX**	E	OM
94147	(86091, 95147)	**RX**	E	ML
94148	(86416, 95148)	**RX**	E	ER
94150	(86560, 95150)	**RX**	E	*E*	ML
94153	(86798, 95153)	**RX**	E	WE

94155	(86820, 95155)	**RX** E	*E*	ML
94157	(86523, 95157)	**RX** E		OM
94160	(86581, 95160)	**RX** E		ML
94164	(86104, 95164)	**RX** E		ML
94166	(86112, 95166)	**RX** E	*E*	ML
94168	(86914, 95168)	**RX** E		TY
94170	(86395, 95170)	**RX** E	*E*	ML
94172	(86429, 95172)	**RX** E		ML
94174	(86852, 95174)	**RX** E		WE
94175	(86521, 95175)	**RX** E		MO
94176	(86210, 95176)	**RX** E	*E*	ML
94177	(86411, 95177)	**RX** E		SM
94180	(86362, 95141)	**RX** E		ML
94182	(86710, 95182)	**RX** E		TE
94190	(86624, 95350)	**RX** E		BK
94191	(86596, 95351)	**RX** E		TE
94192	(86727, 95352)	**RX** E	*E*	ML
94193	(86514, 95353)	**RX** E		WE
94195	(86375, 95355)	**RX** E	*E*	ML
94196	(86478, 95356)	**RX** E	*E*	ML
94197	(86508, 95357)	**RX** E	*E*	ML
94198	(86195, 95358)	**RX** E		ML
94199	(86854, 95359)	**RX** E		TE
94200	(86207, 95360)	**RX** E		MO
94202	(86563, 95362)	**RX** E		MO
94203	(86345, 95363)	**RX** E	*E*	ML
94204	(86715, 95364)	**RX** E		ER
94205	(86857, 95365)	**RX** E		TE
94207	(86529, 95367)	**RX** E		OM
94208	(86656, 95368)	**RX** E		SM
94209	(86390, 95369)	**RX** E		SD
94211	(86713, 95371)	**RX** E		YN
94212	(86728, 95372)	**RX** E		TY
94213	(86258, 95373)	**RX** E	*E*	ML
94214	(86367, 95374)	**RX** E		TY
94215	(86862, 94077)	**RX** E		TY
94216	(86711, 93711)	**RX** E		YN
94217	(86131, 93131)	**RX** E		ML
94218	(86541, 93541)	**RX** E		TE
94221	(86905, 93905)	**RX** E	*E*	ML
94222	(86474, 93474)	**RX** E		ML
94223	(86660, 93660)	**RX** E		TY
94224	(86273, 93273)	**RX** E		CD
94225	(86849, 93849)	**RX** E		ML
94226	(86525, 93525)	**RX** E		MO
94227	(86585, 93585)	**RX** E		TE
94228	(86511, 93511)	**RX** E		TE
94229	(86720, 93720)	**RX** E	*E*	ML

NAA   PROPELLING CONTROL VEHICLE

Mark 1. Class 307 driving trailers converted for use in propelling mail trains out
of termini. Fitted with roller shutter doors. Equipment fitted for communication
between cab of PCV and locomotive. B5 bogies. ETH 2X.

Lot No. 30206 Eastleigh 1954–56. Converted at Hunslet-Barclay, Kilmarnock
1994–6.

94302	(75124)	**RX** E		TY		94323	(75110)	**RX** E	*E*	ML
94303	(75131)	**RX** E		TY		94324	(75103)	**RX** E		MG
94304	(75107)	**RX** E		ML		94325	(75113)	**RX** E		EN
94305	(75104)	**RX** E		EN		94326	(75123)	**RX** E		TY
94306	(75112)	**RX** E		TY		94327	(75116)	**RX** E		EN
94307	(75127)	**RX** E		SD		94331	(75022)	**RX** E		SD
94308	(75125)	**RX** E	*E*	ML		94332	(75011)	**RX** E		TY
94309	(75130)	**RX** E		EN		94333	(75016)	**RX** E		TY
94310	(75119)	**RX** E		WE		94334	(75017)	**RX** E		CD
94311	(75105)	**RX** E		WE		94335	(75032)	**RX** E		TY
94312	(75126)	**RX** E		MG		94336	(75031)	**RX** E		TY
94313	(75129)	**RX** E		WE		94337	(75029)	**RX** E		WE
94314	(75109)	**RX** E		MG		94338	(75008)	**RX** E		WE
94315	(75132)	**RX** E		Rugby		94339	(75024)	**RX** E		TD
94316	(75108)	**RX** E		SM		94340	(75012)	**RX** E		CD
94317	(75117)	**RX** E		OM		94341	(75007)	**RX** E		EN
94318	(75115)	**RX** E		SD		94342	(75005)	**RX** E		EN
94319	(75128)	**RX** E		EN		94343	(75027)	**RX** E		ML
94320	(75120)	**RX** E		Norwich		94344	(75014)	**RX** E		SM
94321	(75122)	**RX** E		EN		94345	(75004)	**RX** E		EN
94322	(75111)	**RX** E		ML						

NBA   HIGH SECURITY BRAKE VAN (100 m.p.h.)

Mark 1. These vehicles are NEs further modified with sealed gangways, new
floors, built-in tail lights and roller shutter doors. For lot Nos. see original number series. B4 bogies. 31.4 t. ETH 1X.

94400	(81224, 92954)	**RX**	E		SD
94401	(81277, 92224)	**RX**	E	*E*	ML
94403	(81479, 92629)	**RX**	E		ML
94404	(81486, 92135)	**RX**	E		MG
94405	(80890, 92233)	**RX**	E		EN
94406	(81226, 92956)	**RX**	E	*E*	ML
94407	(81223, 92553)	**RX**	E		MG
94408	(81264, 92981)	**RX**	E		TY
94410	(81205, 92941)	**RX**	E		WE
94411	(81378, 92997)	**RX**	E		SD
94412	(81210, 92945)	**RX**	E		ML
94413	(80909, 92236)	**RX**	E	*E*	ML
94414	(81377, 92996)	**RX**	E		EN
94415	(81309, 92992)	**RX**	E		YN

94416	(80929, 92746)	**RX**	E		TY
94418	(81248, 92244)	**RX**	E		EN
94420	(81325, 92263)	**RX**	E		ML
94422	(81516, 92651)	**RX**	E		OM
94423	(80923, 92914)	**RX**	E	*E*	ML
94424	(81400, 92103)	**RX**	E		ML
94427	(80894, 92754)	**RX**	E		WE
94428	(81550, 92166)	**RX**	E		ML
94429	(80870, 92232)	**RX**	E		TE
94431	(81401, 92604)	**RX**	E		MO
94432	(81383, 92999)	**RX**	E		TY
94433	(81495, 92643)	**RX**	E		AC
94434	(81268, 92584)	**RX**	E		TY
94435	(81485, 92134)	**RX**	E		WE
94436	(81237, 92565)	**RX**	E		EN
94437	(81403, 92208)	**RX**	E		EN
94438	(81425, 92251)	**RX**	E		YN
94439	(81480, 92130)	**RX**	E		ER
94440	(81497, 92645)	**RX**	E		TY
94441	(81492, 92140)	**RX**	E		ML
94442	(80932, 92723)	**RX**	E		ER
94443	(81473, 92127)	**RX**	E		ML
94444	(81484, 92133)	**RX**	E		ML
94445	(81444, 92615)	**RX**	E		WE
94446	(80857, 92242)	**RX**	E		ER
94447	(81515, 92266)	**RX**	E		EN
94448	(81541, 92664)	**RX**	E		TY
94449	(81536, 92747)	**RX**	E		SD
94450	(80927, 92915)	**RX**	E		WE
94451	(80955, 92257)	**RX**	E		WE
94452	(81394, 92602)	**RX**	E		YN
94453	(81170, 92239)	**RX**	E		MO
94454	(81465, 92124)	**RX**	E		WE
94455	(81239, 92264)	**RX**	E		SD
94458	(81255, 92974)	**RX**	E		SD
94459	(81490, 92138)	**RX**	E		ML
94460	(81266, 92983)	**RX**	E		ML
94461	(81487, 92136)	**RX**	E		TY
94462	(81289, 92270)	**RX**	E		CD
94463	(81375, 92995)	**RX**	E		TY
94464	(81240, 92262)	**RX**	E		TY
94465	(81481, 92131)	**RX**	E		TY
94466	(81236, 92964)	**RX**	E		WE
94467	(81245, 92969)	**RX**	E		EN
94468	(81259, 92978)	**RX**	E		ML
94469	(81260, 92979)	**RX**	E		TY
94470	(81442, 92113)	**RX**	E		OM
94471	(81518, 92152)	**RX**	E		ER
94472	(81256, 92975)	**RX**	E		ML
94473	(81262, 92272)	**RX**	E		TY
94474	(81452, 92618)	**RX**	E		ML

94475	(81208, 92943)		**RX**	E		TY
94476	(81209, 92944)		**RX**	E		CD
94477	(81494, 92642)		**RX**	E		TY
94478	(81488, 92637)		**RX**	E		TY
94479	(81482, 92132)		**RX**	E		OM
94480	(81411, 92608)		**RX**	E		ML
94481	(81493, 92641)		**RX**	E		SD
94482	(81491, 92639)		**RX**	E		ML
94483	(81500, 92647)		**RX**	E		SD
94484	(81426, 92110)		**RX**	E		EN
94485	(81496, 92644)		**RX**	E		SD
94486	(81254, 92973)		**RX**	E		ML
94487	(81413, 92609)		**RX**	E		ML
94488	(81405, 92105)		**RX**	E		CD
94490	(81409, 92606)		**RX**	E		MO
94492	(80888, 92721)		**RX**	E		WE
94493	(80944, 92919)		**RX**	E		YN
94494	(81451, 92617)		**RX**	E		EN
94495	(80871, 92755)		**RX**	E		TY
94496	(81514, 92650)		**RX**	E		EN
94497	(80877, 92717)		**RX**	E		ML
94498	(81225, 92555)		**RX**	E		MO
94499	(81258, 92577)		**RX**	E		CD

NBA/NIA/NQA
HIGH SECURITY BRAKE VAN (100/110 m.p.h.)

Mark 1. These vehicles are NEs further modified with sealed gangways, new floors, built-in tail lights and roller shutter doors. For lot Nos. see original number series. B4 bogies. 31.4 t. ETH 1X.

These vehicles are identical to the 94400–94499 series. Certain vehicles are being given a special maintenance regime whereby tyres are reprofiled more frequently than normal and are then allowed to run at 110 m.p.h. Vehicles from the 94400 series upgraded to 110 m.p.h. are being renumbered in this series. Vehicles are NBA (100 m.p.h.) unless marked NIA or NQA (110 m.p.h.). NQA are vehicles which were modified for haulage by Class 90/2 locomotives which were fitted with composition brake blocks.

94500	(81457, 92121)	NIA	**RX**	E		OM
94501	(80891, 92725)		**RX**	E		OM
94502	(80924, 92720)	NQA	**RX**	E		ML
94503	(80873, 92709)	NIA	**RX**	E		SD
94504	(80935, 92748)	NQA	**RX**	E	*E*	ML
94505	(81235, 92750)	NIA	**RX**	E		YN
94506	(80958, 92922)	NIA	**RX**	E		MO
94507	(80876, 92505)	NIA	**RX**	E		YN
94508	(80887, 92722)	NQA	**RX**	E		ML
94509	(80897, 92509)	NQA	**RX**	E		OM
94510	(80945, 92265)		**RX**	E		WE
94511	(81504, 92714)	NIA	**RX**	E		OM

94512	(81265, 92582)		**RX**	E		TY
94513	(81257, 92576)		**RX**	E		YN
94514	(81459, 92122)	NIA	**RX**	E		TY
94515	(80916, 92513)	NQA	**RX**	E		MO
94516	(81267, 92211)	NQA	**RX**	E		TY
94517	(81489, 92243)	NIA	**RX**	E		CD
94518	(81346, 92258)		**RX**	E		ML
94519	(80930, 92916)	NQA	**RX**	E		OM
94520	(80940, 92917)	NQA	**RX**	E		TY
94521	(80900, 92510)	NIA	**RX**	E		CD
94522	(80880, 92907)	NIA	**RX**	E		TY
94523	(81509, 92649)	NIA	**RX**	E		EN
94524	(81454, 94457)	NQA	**RX**	E		SD
94525	(80902, 92229)	NIA	**RX**	E		TY
94526	(80941, 92518)	NIA	**RX**	E		TY
94527	(80921, 92728)	NQA	**RX**	E		TY
94528	(81404, 92267)		**RX**	E	E	ML
94529	(80959, 92252)	NQA	**RX**	E		CD
94530	(81511, 94409)	NIA	**RX**	E		TY
94531	(80879, 94456)	NQA	**RX**	E		TY
94532	(81423, 94489)	NQA	**RX**	E		OM
94534	(80908, 94430)	NIA	**RX**	E		TY
94535	(80858, 94419)	NIA	**RX**	E		EN
94536	(80936, 94491)	NIA	**RX**	E	E	ML
94537	(81230, 94421)	NIA	**RX**	E		MG
94538	(81283, 94426)	NQA	**RX**	E		MO

NBA HIGH SECURITY BRAKE VAN (100 m.p.h.)

Mark 1. Details as for 94400–99 but fitted with Commonwealth bogies. 34.4 t. ETH 1X.

94539	(81501, 92302)	**RX**	E	E	ML
94540	(81431, 92860)	**RX**	E		TJ
94541	(80980, 92316)	**RX**	E	E	ML
94542	(80995, 92330)	**RX**	E		TY
94543	(81026, 92389)	**RX**	E		MO
94544	(81083, 92345)	**RX**	E		MO
94545	(81001, 92329)	**RX**	E		TE
94546	(81339, 92804)	**RX**	E		TY
94547	(80861, 92392)	**RX**	E		MO
94548	(81154, 92344)	**RX**	E		TY

NRA   BAA CONTAINER VAN (100 m.p.h.)

Mark 1. Modified for carriage of British Airports Authority containers with roller shutter doors and roller floors and gangways removed. Now used for general parcels traffic. For lot Nos. see original number series. Commonwealth bogies. Add 2 t to weight. ETH3.

| 95400 | (80621, 95203) | **E** | E | E | ML |
| 95410 | (80826, 95213) | **E** | E | E | ML |

NOA HIGH SECURITY GENERAL UTILITY VAN

Mark 1. These vehicles are GUVs further modified with new floors, two roller shutter doors per side, middle doors sealed and end doors removed. For lot Nos. see original number series. Commonwealth bogies. Add 2 t to weight. ETH 0X.

95715	(86174, 95115)	**R**	E	TY
95727	(86323, 95127)	**R**	E	WE
95734	(86462, 95134)	**R**	E	EN
95739	(86172, 95139)	**R**	E	WE
95743	(86485, 95143)	**R**	E	EN
95749	(86265, 95149)	**R**	E	TY
95754	(86897, 95154)	**R**	E	TY
95758	(86499, 95158)	**R**	E	TY
95759	(86084, 95159)	**R**	E	EN
95761	(86205, 95161)	**R**	E	WE
95762	(86122, 95162)	**R**	E	WE
95763	(86407, 95163)	**R**	E	TY

NP/NX/NV (GUV) MOTORAIL VAN (100 m.p.h.)

Mark 1. For details and lot numbers see original number series. ETH 0 (0X*).

Notes:

96100 was authorised for 110 m.p.h. and is classified NP.
96101 has a new prototype body built 1998 by Marcroft Engineering with side loading and one end sealed and is classified NV.

96100	(86734, 93734)	*B5		H		TM
96101	(86741, 93741)	*B5	**HB**	H		PY
96132	(86754, 93754)	*C		H		LT
96139	(86751, 93751)	C		H	*VW*	MA
96164	(86880, 93880)	*C		H		LT
96181	(86875, 93875)	*C		H		KT

AX5G NIGHTSTAR GENERATOR VAN

Mark 3A. Generator vans converted from sleeping cars for use on 'Nightstar' services. Designed to operate between two Class 37/6 locomotives. Gangways removed. Two Cummins diesel generator groups providing a 1500 V train supply. Hydraulic parking brake. 61-way ENS interface jumpers. BT10 bogies.

Lot No. 30960 Derby 1981–83. 46.01 t.

96371	(10545, 6371)	**EP**	EU	NP
96372	(10564, 6372)	**EP**	EU	NP
96373	(10568, 6373)	**EP**	EU	NP
96374	(10585, 6374)	**EP**	EU	NP
96375	(10587, 6375)	**EP**	EU	NP

AY5 (BV)   EUROSTAR BARRIER VEHICLE

Mark 1. Converted from GUVs. Bodies removed. B4 bogies.

96380–96382. Lot No. 30417 Pressed Steel 1958–59. 40 t.
96383. Lot No. 30565 Pressed Steel 1959. 40 t.
96384. Lot No. 30616 Pressed Steel 1959–60. 40 t.

96380	(86386, 6380)	**B**	EU	*EU*	NP
96381	(86187, 6381)	**B**	EU	*EU*	NP
96382	(86295, 6382)	**B**	EU	*EU*	NP
96383	(86664, 6383)	**B**	EU	*EU*	NP
96384	(86955, 6384)	**B**	EU	*EU*	NP

NVA   MOTORAIL VAN (100 m.p.h.)

Mark 1. Built 1998–9 by Marcroft Engineering using underframe and running gear from Motorail GUVs. Side loading with one end sealed. The vehicles run in pairs and access is available to the adjacent vehicle. For details and lot numbers see original number series. B5 bogies. ETH 0X.

96602	(86097, 96150)	**GL**	H	*GW*	PZ
96603	(86334, 96155)	**GL**	H	*GW*	PZ
96604	(86337, 96156)	**GL**	H	*GW*	PZ
96605	(86344, 96157)	**GL**	H	*GW*	PZ
96606	(86324, 96213)	**GL**	H	*GW*	PZ
96607	(86351, 96215)	**GL**	H	*GW*	PZ
96608	(86385, 96216)	**GL**	H	*GW*	PZ
96609	(86327, 96217)	**GL**	H	*GW*	PZ

NY   ULTRASONIC TEST COACH

Converted Railway Age, Crewe 1996 from FO to Exhibition Van. Further converted at Alstom, Wolverton Works 2002 to Ultrasonic Test Coach. B4 bogies.

Lot No. 30843 Derby 1972–73.

99666	(3250)	**RK**	NR	*SO*	ZA

YR   FERRY VAN

This vehicle was built to a wagon lot although the design closely resembles that of NJ except it only has two sets of doors per side. Short Frames (57'). Load 14 t. Commonwealth bogies.

Built Eastleigh 1958. Wagon Lot. No. 2849. 30 t.

Non-Standard Livery: 889202 is Pullman Car umber with gold lining and lettering.

889202		**0**	VS	CP

Name: 889202 is branded 'BAGGAGE CAR No.8'.

EWS Silver-liveried DVT 82146 and EWS Maroon-liveried Mark 3A SLEP 10546 forming part of the EWS Executive Train are seen at Bathampton on 08/06/05. The other vehicles usually in this train are 11039, 10211 and 67029. **John Chalcraft**

▲ VSOE Northern Belle-liveried Mark 3A Sleeping Car 10729 "CREWE", usually formed in the "Northern Belle" luxury train, is seen at Worcester Shrub Hill on 10/07/04. **Stephen Widdowson**

▼ GNER-liveried HST TRFB 40711 is seen at Edinburgh Waverley on 15/07/05. **Robert Pritchard**

▲ Midland Mainline-liveried HST TF 41117 is in the unusual location, for an HST, of Lincoln Central station on 04/12/04. The MML HST set was on hire to Central Trains for the day for working services between Lincoln and Nottingham in connection with the Lincoln Christmas Market. **Robert Pritchard**

▼ First Great Western-liveried HST TS 42293 at Totnes on 16/07/05.
Robert Pritchard

▲ Refurbished GNER-liveried "Mallard" Mark 4 TSO 12405 passes Newark North Gate on 11/12/04.   **Stephen Widdowson**

▼ VSOE Pullman car-liveried Kitchen First No. 284 "VERA", with B5 (SR) bogies, at Cardiff Central on 29/06/02.   **Ivor Bufton**

▲ Network Rail-liveried Mark 1 Generator Van 6260 and another vehicle in Network Rail yellow livery are seen at Worting Junction on 24/06/05.

Darren Ford

▼ BR Blue-liveried Mark 1 Generator Van 6311 at Havant on 27/03/04.

Darren Ford

Rail Charter Services

▲ Porterbrook-liveried Mark 1 EMU Translator Vehicle 6379 at Bedford on 04/09/04.   **Mark Beal**

▼ Network Rail Yellow-liveried Overhead Line Equipment Test Coach 975091 (also known as "MENTOR" and converted from a Mark 1) at Derby on 03/06/05.
                                                                    Robert Pritchard

▲ Serco Railtest-liveried Test Coach 975290, converted from a Mark 2, at RTC Business Park Derby on 26/09/04. **Paul Robertson**

▼ Refurbished Overhead Line Maintenance, stores & roof access coach 975733, converted from a Mark 1, at Rugby Rail Plant depot on 31/12/04. **Mark Beal**

▲ Newly converted Network Rail Yellow-liveried HST New Measurement Train vehicle 977995 (converted from TRFM 40619) at RTC Business Park, Derby on 03/07/05. **Paul Robertson**

▼ BR Maroon-liveried Inspection Coach 999506 "AMANDA", converted from a BR Inspection Saloon, is seen at RTC Business Park, Derby on 03/07/05. **Paul Robertson**

9. NPCCS AWAITING DISPOSAL

80211	DY	80371	MG	80430	EN
80319	ER	80372	TJ	80431	EN
80320	EN	80373	EN	80432	TO
80321	EN	80374	WE	80433	EN
80322	SD	80375	EN	80434	TO
80323	EN	80376	WE	80435	EN
80324	WE	80377	EN	80436	ER
80325	WE	80378	EN	80437	EN
80326	EN	80379	EN	80438	EN
80327	EN	80380	EN	80439	MG
80331	EN	80381	WE	80456	EN
80332	WE	80382	EN	80457	EN
80333	TJ	80383	WE	80458	EN
80334	WE	80384	TJ	80865	Hornsey Sand Terminal
80337	EN	80385	EN	84364	DW
80339	EN	80386	SD	84519	CD
80340	TJ	80387	YN	92114	DY
80341	ER	80390	YN	92146	DY
80342	ER	80392	ER	92193	Preston Carriage Sidings
80343	WE	80393	WE	92198	ZB
80344	EN	80394	EN	92303	OM
80345	EN	80395	EN	92314	CD
80346	EN	80400	MG	92321	FP
80347	EN	80401	TO	92350	OM
80348	WE	80402	EN	92400	CD
80349	EN	80403	WE	92530	OM
80350	EN	80404	WE	92939	DY
80351	EN	80405	WE	93180	Derby South Dock Siding
80352	EN	80406	TJ	93446	CD
80353	ER	80411	ER	93723	Bletchley T&RSMD
80354	EN	80412	ER	93930	CD
80355	ER	80413	WE	94027	FP
80356	EN	80414	EN	95228	NC
80357	SD	80415	ER	95300	ML
80358	EN	80416	TJ	95301	ML
80359	EN	80417	EN	96110	CS
80360	EN	80419	EN	96135	CS
80361	EN	80420	ER	96165	CS
80362	ER	80421	WE	96170	CS
80363	EN	80422	SD	96175	CS
80364	SD	80423	EN	96177	CP
80365	EN	80424	SD	96178	CS
80366	WE	80425	TJ	96182	CS
80367	EN	80426	EN	96191	CS
80368	EN	80427	EN	96192	CS
80369	SD	80428	EN	96210	AS
80370	YN	80429	EN	96212	AS

| 96218 | AS | 96453 | BR | 99646 | FP |
| 96452 | BR | 99645 | FP | | |

10. SERVICE STOCK

Vehicles in this section are numbered in the former BR departmental number series. They are used for internal purposes within the railway industry, i.e. they do not generate revenue from outside the industry.

EMU TRANSLATOR VEHICLES

These vehicles are used to move EMU vehicles around the National Rail system in the same way as other vehicles included in this book. Similar vehicles numbered in the BR capital stock series are included elsewhere in this book. Converted from Mark 1 TSO, RSOs, RUOs, BSKs and GUVs (NP/NL).

975864. Lot No. 30054 Eastleigh 1951–54. Commonwealth bogies.
975867. Lot No. 30014 York 1950–51. Commonwealth bogies.
975875. Lot No. 30143 Charles Roberts 1954–55. Commonwealth bogies.
975974–975978. Lot No. 30647 Wolverton 1959–61. Commonwealth bogies.
977087. Lot No. 30229 Metro–Cammell 1955–57. Commonwealth bogies.
977942/948. Lot No. 30417 Pressed Steel 1958–59. B5 bogies.
977943/949. Lot No. 30565 Pressed Steel 1959. B5 bogies.

Non-standard livery: 975974 and 975978 are in plain grey.

975864	(3849)	**HB**	H	*FL*	ZJ
975867	(1006)	**HB**	H	*FL*	ZJ
975875	(34643)	**HB**	H	*FL*	ZJ
975974	(1030)	**0**	A	*ME*	BD
975976	(1033)	**N**	A		KT
975977	(1023)	**N**	A		KT
975978	(1025)	**0**	A	*ME*	BD
977087	(34971)	**HB**	H	*FL*	ZJ
977942	(86467, 80251)	**E**	E	*E*	TO
977943	(86718, 80252)	**E**	E	*E*	TO
977948	(86733, 94028)	**E**	E	*E*	TO
977949	(86377, 94025)	**E**	E	*E*	TO

LABORATORY, TESTING & INSTRUCTION COACHES

These coaches are used for research, development, instruction, testing and inspection on the National Rail system. Many are fitted with sophisticated technical equipment.

Structure Gauging Driving Trailer Coach. Converted from BR Mark 1 BSK. Lot No. 30699 Wolverton 1961–63. B4 bogies.

975081	(35313)	**Y**	NR	*SO*	ZA

Overhead Line Equipment Test Coach. Can either be locomotive hauled or included between DMU vehicles 977391/2. Converted from BR Mark 1 BSK Lot No. 30142 Gloucester 1954–5. B4 bogies.

975091	(34615)	**Y**	NR	*SO*	ZA

Structure Gauging Train Dormitory and Generator Coach. Converted from BR Mark 1 BCK Lot No. 30732 Derby 1962–4. B4 bogies.

975280 (21263) **Y** NR *SO* ZA

Test Coach. Converted from BR Mark 2 FK Lot No. 30734 Derby 1962–64. B4 bogies.

975290 (13396) **SO** SO *SO* ZA

Test Coach. Converted from BR Mark 1 BSK Lot No. 30699 Wolverton 1961–63. Commonwealth bogies.

975397 (35386) **SO** SO *SO* ZA

Cinema Coach. Converted from BR Mark 1 TSO Lot No. 30243 York 1955–57. BR Mark 1 bogies.

975403 (4598) **FG** FG *GW* PM

Test Coach. Converted from BR Mark 1 BSK Lot No. 30223 Charles Roberts 1955–56. BT5 bogies.

975422 (34875) **SO** SO *SO* ZA

New Measurement Train Conference Coach. Converted from prototype HST TF Lot No. 30848 Derby 1972. BT10 bogies.

975814 (11000,41000) **Y** NR *SO* EC

New Measurement Train Lecture Coach. Converted from prototype HST TRUB Lot No. 30849 Derby 1972–3. BT10 bogies.

975984 (10000, 40000) **Y** NR *SO* EC

Track Recording Train Dormitory Coach. Converted from BR Mark 2 BSO. Lot No 30757 Derby 1965–66. B4 bogies.

977337 (9395) **Y** NR *SO* ZA

Track Recording Train Brake & Stores Coach. Converted from Mark 2 BSO. Lot No. 30757 Derby 1965–66. B4 bogies.

977338 (9387) **SO** SO *SO* ZA

Radio Equipment Survey Coaches. Converted from BR Mark 2E TSO. Lot No. 30844 Derby 1972–73. B4 bogies.

977868 (5846) **RK** NR *SO* ZA
977869 (5858) **RK** NR *SO* ZA

Test Train Staff Coach. Converted from Royal Household couchette Lot No. 30889, which in turn had been converted from BR Mark 2B BFK Lot No. 30790 Derby 1969. B5 bogies.

977969 (14112, 2906) **Y** NR *SO* ZA

New Measurement Train Laboratory Coach. Converted from BR Mark 2E TSO. Lot No. 30844 Derby 1972–73. B4 bogies.

977974 (5854) **Y** AE *SO* ZA

Hot Box Detection Coach. Converted from BR Mark 2F FO converted to Class 488/2 EMU TFOH. Lot No. 30859 Derby 1973–74. B4 bogies.

977983 (3407, 72503)   RK   NR   *SO*   ZA

New Measurement Train Staff Coach. Converted from HST TRFK. Lot No. 30884 Derby 1976–77. BT10 bogies.

977984 (40501)   **Y**   P   *SO*   EC

Structure Gauging Train Coach. Converted from BR Mark 2F TSO converted to Class 488/3 EMU TSO. Lot No. 30860 Derby 1973–74. B4 bogies.

977985 (6019, 72715)   **Y**   NR   *SO*   ZA

Structure Gauging Train Coach. Converted from BR Mark 2D FO subsequently declassified to SO and then converted to exhibition van. Lot No. 30821 Derby 1971.

977986 (3189, 99664)   **Y**   NR   *SO*   ZA

New Measurement Train Overhead Line Equipment Test Coach. Converted from HST TGS. Lot No. 30949 Derby 1982. BT10 bogies.

977993 (44053)   **Y**   P   *SO*   EC

New Measurement Train Laboratory Coach. Converted from HST TGS. Lot No. 30949 Derby 1982. BT10 bogies.

977994 (44087)   **Y**   P   *SO*   EC

New Measurement Train Coach. Converted from HST TRFM. Lot No. 30921 Derby 1978–79. BT10 bogies.

977995 (40719, 40619)   **Y**   P   *SO*   EC

Inspection Coach. Converted from BR Inspection Saloon. BR Wagon Lot No. 3095. Swindon 1957. B4 bogies.

999506 AMANDA   **M**   NR   *SO*   ZA

Track Recording Coach. Converted from BR Inspection Saloon. BR Wagon Lot No. 3379. Swindon 1960. B4 bogies.

999508   **SO**   SO   *SO*   ZA

New Measurement Train Track Recording Coach. Purpose built Mark 2. B4 bogies.

999550   **Y**   NR   *SO*   EC

TEST TRAIN BRAKE FORCE RUNNERS

These vehicles are included in test trains to provide brake force and are not used for any other purposes. Other vehicles included in this book may also be similarly used on a temporary basis if required. Converted from BR Mark 2 TSOs and BFKs.

977468/470/801/2. Lot No. 30751 Derby 1964–7. B4 bogies.
977789. Lot No. 30837 Derby 1971–72. B4 bogies.
977790/1. Lot No. 30844 Derby 1972–73. B4 bogies.
977793. Lot No. 30795 Derby 1969–70. B4 bogies.
977794. Lot No. 30823 Derby 1969–72. B4 bogies.

Non-Standard Liveries: 977789–94 are Adtranz White with yellow stripe.

977468	(5169)	**SO**	SO	*SO*	ZA
977470	(5134)	**SO**	SO	*SO*	ZA
977789	(5765)	**O**	FM		LU
977790	(5830)	**O**	FM		LU
977791	(5855)	**O**	FM		LU
977793	(5596)	**O**	FM		LU
977794	(14139, 17139)	**O**	FM		LU
977801	(5153)	**SO**	SO	*SO*	ZA
977802	(5176)	**SO**	SO	*SO*	ZA

BREAKDOWN TRAIN COACHES

These coaches are formed in trains used for the recovery of derailed railway vehicles and were converted from BR Mark 1 BCK, BG, BSK and SK. The current use of each vehicle is given. 975611–613 were previously converted to trailer luggage vans in 1968. BR Mark 1 bogies.

975080. Lot No. 30155 Wolverton 1955–56.
975087. Lot No. 30032 Wolverton 1951–52.
975463/573. Lot No. 30156 Wolverton 1954–55.
975465/477/494. Lot No. 30233 GRCW 1955–57.
975471. Lot No. 30095 Wolverton 1953–55.
975481/482/574. Lot No. 30141 GRCW 1954–55.
975498. Lot No. 30074 Wolverton 1953–54.
975611–613. Lot No. 30162 Pressed Steel 1954–57.
977088/235. Lot No. 30229 Metro-Cammell 1955–57.
977107. Lot No. 30425 Metro-Cammell 1956–58.

r refurbished

975080	(25079)	r	**Y**	NR	*E*	TO	Tool Van
975087	(34289)	r	**NR**	NR	*E*	LU	Generator Van
975463	(34721)	r	**Y**	NR	*E*	TE	Staff Coach
975465	(35109)	r	**Y**	NR	*E*	TO	Staff Coach
975471	(34543)	r	**NR**	NR	*E*	LU	Staff & Tool Coach
975477	(35108)	r	**NR**	NR	*E*	LU	Staff Coach
975481	(34606)	r	**Y**	NR	*E*	TO	Generator Van
975482	(34602)	r	**Y**	NR	*E*	TE	Generator Van
975494	(35082)	r	**Y**	NR	*E*	MG	Generator Van
975498	(34367)	r	**Y**	NR	*E*	TE	Tool Van
975573	(34729)	r	**Y**	NR	*E*	MG	Staff Coach
975574	(34599)	r	**Y**	NR	*E*	OM	Staff Coach
975611	(80915, 68201)	r	**Y**	NR	*E*	OM	Generator Van
975612	(80922, 68203)	r	**Y**	NR	*E*	MG	Tool Van
975613	(80918, 68202)	r	**Y**	NR	*E*	OM	Tool Van
977088	(34990)		**Y**	NR	*E*	CE	Generator Van
977107	(21202)		**Y**	NR	*E*	CE	Staff Coach
977235	(34989, 083172)		**Y**	NR	*E*	CE	Tool Van

Note: 975087/471/477 are currently in use on the Southern Power upgrade Project.

INFRASTRUCTURE MAINTENANCE COACHES

Overhead Line Maintenance Coaches

These coaches are formed in trains used for the maintenance, repair and renewal of overhead lines and were converted from BR Mark 1 BSK, CK and SK. The current use of each vehicle is given. All have been refurbished.

Non-standard livery: 975697/698/713/723/733/743 are light grey with red stripe, 975699/700/714/724/734/744 are light grey with blue stripe.

975697/698, 975700. Lot No. 30025 Wolverton 1950–52. BR Mark 1 bogies.
975699. Lot No. 30233 GRCW 1955–57. BR Mark 1 bogies.
975713/744. Lot No. 30350 Wolverton 1956–57. BR Mark 1 bogies.
975714. Lot No. 30374. York 1958. Commonwealth bogies.
975723/743. Lot No. 30349 Wolverton 1956–57. BR Mark 1 bogies.
975724. Lot No. 30471 Metro-Cammell 1957–59. Commonwealth bogies.
975733. Lot No. 30351 Wolverton 1956–57. BR Mark 1 bogies.
975734. Lot No. 30426 Wolverton 1956–58. BR Mark 1 Bogies.

975697	(34147)	0	CA	*CA*	RU	Pantograph coach
975698	(34148)	0	CA	*CA*	RU	Pantograph coach
975699	(35105)	0	CA	*CA*	Preston	Pantograph coach
975700	(34138)	0	CA	*CA*	Preston	Pantograph coach
975713	(25420)	0	CA	*CA*	RU	Stores van
975714	(25466)	0	CA	*CA*	Preston	Stores van
975723	(25388)	0	CA	*CA*	RU	Stores & generator van
975724	(16079)	0	CA	*CA*	Preston	Stores & generator van
975733	(16001)	0	CA	*CA*	RU	Stores & roof access coach
975734	(25695)	0	CA	*CA*	Preston	Stores & roof access coach
975743	(25358)	0	CA	*CA*	RU	Staff & office coach
975744	(25440)	0	CA	*CA*	Preston	Staff & office coach

Snowblower Train Coaches

These coaches work with Snowblower ADB 968501. They were converted from BR Mark 1 BSK. The current use of each vehicle is given. Commonwealth bogies.

975464. Lot No. 30386 Charles Roberts 1956–58.
975486. Lot No. 30025 Wolverton 1950–52.

975464	(35171)	Y	NR	*E*	ZK	Staff & dormitory coach
975486	(34100)	Y	NR	*E*	ZK	Tool van

Snowblower Train Tool Vans

These vans work with Snowblower ADB 968500.

200715. Wagon Lot No. 3855 Ashford 1976. 4-wheeled.
787395. Wagon Lot No. 3567 Eastleigh 1966. 4-wheeled.

200715	Y	NR	*E*	IS
787395	Y	NR	*E*	IS

Severn Tunnel Emergency Train Coaches

These coaches were formed in a train used in the event of incidents in the Severn Tunnel. They were converted from BR Mark 1 BSK & BG. The use of each vehicle is given. 975615 was previously converted to a trailer luggage van in 1968.

975497. Lot No. 30427 Wolverton 1956–59. BR Mark 1 bogies.
975615. Lot No. 30162 Pressed Steel 1954–57. BR Mark 1 bogies.
977526. Lot No. 30229 Metro-Cammell 1955–57. Commonwealth bogies.

975497	(35218)	**Y**	NR	Sudbrook	Tool & generator van
975615	(80951, 68206)	**Y**	NR	SJ	Tool van
977526	(35010)	**BG**	NR	SJ	Emergency casualty coach

Spray Coaches

These coaches are used to spray various concoctions onto the rails or trackbed. In addition to spraying equipment they contain storage tanks. They were converted from BR Mark 1 RMB & GUV.

99019. Lot No. 30702 Wolverton 1961–62. Commonwealth bogies.
99025/26. Lot No. 30565 Pressed Steel 1959. B5 bogies.
99027. Lot No. 30417 Pressed Steel 1958–59. B5 bogies.

99019	(1870)	**NR**	NR	*E*	ZA
99025	(86744, 96103)	**RK**	NR		KT
99026	(86745, 96211)	**RK**	NR		KT
99027	(86331, 96214)	**RK**	NR		KT

Miscellaneous Infrastructure Coaches

These coaches are used for various infrastructure projects on National Rail. They were converted from BR Mark 1 BSK & BG, BR Mark 2 BFK and BR Mark 3 SLEP. The current use of each vehicle is given.

977163/165/166. Lot No. 30721 Wolverton 1961–63. Commonwealth bogies.
977167. Lot No. 30699 Wolverton 1961–63. Commonwealth bogies.
977168. Lot No. 30573 GRCW 1959–60. B4 bogies.
977591. Lot No. 30756 Derby 1965–66. B4 bogies.
977989. Lot No. 30960 Derby 1981–83. BT 10 bogies.
977990. Lot No. 30228 Metro-Cammell 1957-58. B4 bogies.
977991. Lot No. 30323 Pressed steel 1957. B4 bogies.

Non-standard liveries:

977163 and167 are white with a blue stripe.
977165, 975166 and 975168 are all over white.
977591 is red and yellow.

977163	(35487)	**O**	BB	*BB*	AP	Staff & generator coach
977165	(35408)	**O**	BB	*BB*	AP	Staff & generator coach
977166	(35419)	**O**	BB	*BB*	AP	Staff & generator coach
977167	(35400)	**O**	BB	*BB*	AP	Staff & generator coach
977168	(35289)	**O**	BB	*BB*	AP	Staff & generator coach
977591	(14033, 17033)	**O**	E	*E*	Newport	Staff & tool coach
977989	(10536)	**M**	J	*J*	Washwood Heath	Staff & Dormitory Coach
977990	(81165, 92937)	**NR**	NR	*E*	LU	Tool Van
977991	(81308, 92991)	**NR**	NR	*E*	LU	Tool Van

INTERNAL USER VEHICLES

These vehicles are confined to yards and depots or do not normally move at all.
Details are given of the internal user number, type and former identity, current
use and location. Many of these listed no longer see regular use.

024709	BR fish van 87122	Stores van	Wembley heavy repair shop
024710	BR fish van 87146	Stores van	Wembley heavy repair shop
024711	BR fish van 87227	Stores van	Wembley heavy repair shop
024877	BR CCT 94698	Stores van	Wavertree Yard,Edge Hill
024909	BR BSOT 9106	Staff accommodation	Preston Station
024953	BR GUV 93682	Stores van	DY
025000	BR BSO 9423	Staff accommodation	Preston Station
025026	BR TSO 5259	Staff accommodation	Wavertree Yard,Edge Hill
025027	LMS CCT 37210	Stores van	ZA
041379	LMS CCT 35527	Stores van	Leeman Road EY, York
041898	BR BG 84608	Stores van	Leeman Road EY, York
041947	BR GUV 93425	Stores van	IL
041963	LMS milk tank 44047	Storage tank	DR
042154	BR GUV 93975	Stores van	Ipswich Upper Yard
061034	BR CCT 94798	Stores van	Marsh Junction, Bristol
061061	BR CCT 94135	Stores van	Oxford station
061171	BR GUV 93480	Stores van	RG
061223	BR GUV 93714	Stores van	Oxford station
083264	BR TSO 4047	Staff accommodation	Ashford station down sidings
083439	BR CCT 94752	Stores van	WD
083602	BR CCT 94494	Stores van	Three Bridges station
083633	BR GUV 93724	Stores van	BI
083644	BR Ferry Van 889201	Stores van	EH
083650	BR GUV 93100	Stores van	Ashford station down sidings
083664	BR Ferry Van 889203	Stores van	EH
095020	LNER BG 70170	Stores van	Inverness Yard
095030	BR GUV 96140	Stores van	EC

Note: CCT = Covered Carriage Truck (a 4-wheeled van similar to a GUV)

11. SERVICE STOCK AWAITING DISPOSAL

This list contains the last known locations of service vehicles awaiting disposal. The definition of which vehicles are "awaiting disposal" is somewhat vague, but generally speaking these are vehicles of types not now in normal service or vehicles which have been damaged by fire, vandalism or collision.

70220	Western Trading Estate Siding, North Acton	975737	Oxford Hinksey Yard*
99014	Horsham Yard	975747	Oxford Hinksey Yard*
99015	Horsham Yard	975991	CD
320645	Leeman Road EY, York	975995	Wolverhampton Low Level Stn
975000	ZA	977077	Ripple Lane Yard
975051	CD	977085	BH
975379	Leeman Road EY, York	977095	CS
975454	TO	977111	Ripple Lane Yard
975484	CS	977112	Ripple Lane Yard
975491	TH	977169	OM
975535	Carnforth Bottom End Sidings	977182	Eastleigh Down CS
975554	DW	977183	Eastleigh Down CS
975555	DW	977193	BH
975557	Carstairs	977331	BR
975558	Carstairs	977359	ZN
975559	Carstairs	977390	CD
975639	CS	977399	NL
975658	York South Sidings	977449	CD
975680	Carstairs	977510	FP
975681	Portobello	977595	CD
975682	Portobello	977618	BY
975683	Carstairs	977695	Eastleigh Down CS
975684	Carstairs	977787	TH
975685	Portobello	977795	ZN
975686	Portobello	977796	CT
975687	Portobello	977855	ZA
975688	Portobello	977905	EH
975706	Oxford Hinksey Yard*	977944	TO
975717	Oxford Hinksey Yard*	977945	TO
975721	DW	977946	TO
975727	Oxford Hinksey Yard*	977947	TO

* In use as environmental sound protection barrier.

12. CODES

12.1. LIVERY CODES

Coaching stock vehicles are in Inter City (light grey/red stripe/white stripe/ dark grey) livery unless otherwise indicated. The colour of the lower half of the bodyside is stated first.

1   "One" (metallic grey with a broad black bodyside stripe. Pink, yellow, grey, pale green and light blue stripes at the unit/vehicle ends).
AL Advertising livery (see class heading for details).
AR Anglia Railways (turquoise blue with a white stripe).
AV Arriva Trains (turquoise blue with white doors).
B   BR blue.
BG BR blue & grey lined out in white.
CH BR Western Region/GWR (chocolate & cream lined out in gold).
CP First ScotRail Caledonian Sleepers {revised} (all over purple).
CS ScotRail Caledonian Sleepers (two-tone purple with silver stripe).
DR Direct Rail Services (dark blue with light blue or dark grey roof).
E   English Welsh & Scottish Railway (maroon bodyside & roof with gold band).
EP European Passenger Services (two-tone grey with dark blue roof).
FG First Group corporate Inter-City livery (indigo blue with a white roof & gold, pink & white stripes)
FP Old First Great Western (green & ivory with thin green & broad gold stripes).
G   BR Southern Region/SR green.
GC British racing green & cream lined out in gold.
GL First Great Western locos/Motorail vans (green with a gold stripe).
GN Great North Eastern Railway (dark blue with a red stripe).
HB HSBC Rail (Oxford blue & white)
LN LNER Tourist (green & cream).
M   BR maroon (Maroon lined out in straw & black).
MA Maintrain (blue).
MN New Midland Mainline (Thin tangerine stripe on the lower bodyside, ocean blue, grey & white).
N   BR Network South East (white & blue with red lower bodyside stripe, grey solebar & cab ends).
NR Network Rail (blue with a red stripe).
O   Non standard livery (see class heading for details).
P   Porterbrook Leasing Company (purple & grey or white).
PC Pullman Car Company (umber & cream with gold lettering) lined out in gold.
R   Plain red.
RK Railtrack (green and blue or plain blue).
RP Royal Train (claret, lined out in red & black).
RR Regional Railways (dark blue/grey with light blue & white stripes).
RV Riviera Trains (Oxford blue & cream, lined out in gold).
RX Rail Express Systems (dark grey & red with or without blue markings).
SO Serco Railtest (red & grey).

V   Virgin Trains (red with black doors extending into bodysides, three white lower bodyside stripes).
VN Venice Simplon Orient Express "Northern Belle" (crimson lake & cream).
WR Waterman Railways (maroon with cream stripes).
WX Heart of Wessex Line promotional livery (cerise pink with various images.)
Y   Network Rail Yellow.

12.2. OWNER CODES

24	6024 Preservation Society
62	The Princess Royal Locomotive Trust
A	Angel Trains
AE	AEA Technology Rail
B1	Thompson B1 Locomotive Society
BB	Balfour Beatty Rail Plant
BK	The Scottish Railway Preservation Society
BS	Bressingham Steam Museum
CA	Carillion Rail Plant
DG	Duke of Gloucester Steam Locomotive Trust
DR	Direct Rail Services
E	English Welsh & Scottish Railway
EU	Eurostar (UK)
FG	First Group
FM	FM Rail (Fragonset Merlin Railways)
GS	The Great Scottish & Western Railway Company
GW	The Great Western Society
H	HSBC Rail (UK)
HN	Harry Needle Railroad Company
IR	Ian Riley Engineering
J	Fastline
JH	Jeremy Hosking
LW	London & North Western Railway Company
MA	Maintrain
MH	Mid-Hants Railway
MN	Merchant Navy Locomotive Preservation Society
NE	North Eastern Locomotive Preservation Group
NM	National Railway Museum
NR	Network Rail
P	Porterbrook Leasing Company
RA	Railfilms
RP	Rampart Carriage & Wagon Works
RV	Riviera Trains
SH	Scottish Highland Railway Company
SM	Siemens Transportation
SO	Serco Railtest
SV	Severn Valley Railway
VS	Venice-Simplon Orient Express
VT	Vintage Trains
WC	West Coast Railway Company
WT	Wessex Trains

12.3. OPERATOR CODES

The two letter operator codes give the current operator. This is the organisation which facilitates the use of the coach and may not be the actual train operating company which runs the train on which the particular coach is used. If no operator code is shown then the vehicle is not at present in use.

62	The Princes Royal Locomotive Trust
1A	One Anglia
AE	AEA Technology Rail
AW	Arriva Trains Wales
BB	Balfour Beatty Rail Plant
BK	The Scottish Railway Preservation Society
CA	Carillion Rail Plant
CD	Cotswold Rail
CT	Central Trains
DR	Direct Rail Services
E	English Welsh & Scottish Railway
EU	Eurostar (UK)
FL	Freightliner
FM	FM Rail (Fragonset Merlin Railways)
GN	Great North Eastern Railway
GS	The Great Scottish & Western Railway Company
GW	First Great Western
J	Fastline
LS	Locomotive support coach
ME	Merseyrail Electrics
MH	Mid-Hants Railway
MM	Midland Mainline
RA	Railfilms
RP	Royal Train
RV	Riviera Trains
SH	Scottish Highland Railway Company
SO	Serco Railtest
SR	First ScotRail
VS	Venice-Simplon Orient Express
VT	Vintage Trains
VW	Virgin West Coast
VX	Virgin Cross-Country
WC	West Coast Railway Company
WN	(West Anglia) Great Northern
WT	Wessex Trains
WX	Wessex Trains (TOC)

12.4. ALLOCATION & LOCATION CODES

Code	Depot	Operator
AC	Aberdeen Clayhills	*Storage location only*
AP*	Ashford Rail Plant	Balfour Beatty Rail Plant
AS*	Allely's, Studley (Warwickshire)	*Storage location only*

BD	Birkenhead North	Merseyrail Electrics
BH	Barrow Hill (Chesterfield)	Barrow Hill Engine Shed Society
BI	Brighton Lovers Walk	Southern
BK	Bristol Barton Hill	EWS
BN	Bounds Green (London)	GNER
BQ	Bury (Greater Manchester)	East Lancashire Railway/ Ian Riley Engineering
BR*	MoD DSDC Bicester	Ministry of Defence
BT	Bo'ness (West Lothian)	Bo'ness & Kinneil Railway
BY	Bletchley	Silverlink
CD	Crewe Diesel	EWS
CE	Crewe International Electric	EWS
CF	Cardiff Canton	Arriva Trains Wales/Pullman Rail
CJ	Clapham Yard (London)	South West Trains
CO	Cranmore (Somerset)	East Somerset Railway
CP	Crewe Carriage	London & North Western Railway Co.
CS	Carnforth	West Coast Railway Company
CT*	MoD Caerwent AFD (Chepstow)	Ministry of Defence
DI	Didcot Railway Centre	Great Western Society
DR	Doncaster	EWS
DW	Doncaster West Yard	*Storage location only*
DY	Derby Etches Park	Maintrain
EC	Edinburgh Craigentinny	GNER
EH	Eastleigh	EWS
EN	Euston Downside (London)	EWS
ER	Exeter Riverside Yard	*Storage location only*
FP	Ferme Park Sidings	GNER
GW	Shields Road (Glasgow)	First ScotRail
HE	Hornsey (London)	WAGN/"One"
HM	Healey Mills (Wakefield)	EWS
IL	Ilford (London)	"One"
IS	Inverness	First ScotRail
KM	Carlisle Kingmoor	Direct Rail Services
KR	Kidderminster	Severn Valley Railway
KT	MoD Kineton (Warwickshire)	Ministry of Defence
LA	Laira (Plymouth)	First Great Western
LT	MoD Longtown/Smalmstown (Cumbria)	Ministry of Defence
LU	MoD Ludgershall	Ministry of Defence
MA	Manchester Longsight	West Coast Traincare
MG	Margam (Port Talbot)	EWS
ML	Motherwell (Glasgow)	EWS
MM	Fire Service College, Moreton-in-Marsh	Cotswold Rail
MO	Mossend Yard	EWS
MQ	Meldon Quarry (Okehampton)	Dartmoor Railways
NC	Norwich Crown Point	"One"
NL	Neville Hill (Leeds)	Northern/Maintrain
NP	North Pole International (London)	Eurostar (UK)
NY	Grosmont (North Yorkshire)	North Yorkshire Moors Railway
OM	Old Oak Common carriage (London)	Riviera Trains/EWS
OO	Old Oak Common HST (London)	First Great Western
OY	Oxley (Wolverhampton)	West Coast Traincare

PC	Polmadie (Glasgow)	West Coast Traincare
PM	St. Philip's Marsh (Bristol)	First Great Western
PY	MoD DERA Pig's Bay (Shoeburyness)	Ministry of Defence
PZ	Penzance	First Great Western
RD	Nottingham Heritage Centre (Ruddington)	Great Central Railway (North)
RG	Reading	First Great Western Link
RL	Ropley (Hampshire)	Mid-Hants Railway
RU*	Rugby Rail Plant	Carillion Rail Plant
SD	Stoke Gifford Yard (Bristol Parkway)	*Storage location only*
SI	Soho (Birmingham)	Maintrain
SJ	Severn Tunnel Junction	EWS
SK	Swanwick Junction (Derbyshire)	Midland Railway-Butterley
SL	Stewarts Lane (London)	Gatwick Express/VSOE
SM	Swansea Maliphant Sidings	*Storage location only*
SO	Southall (Greater London)	Jeremy Hosking
SW	Swindon STEAM museum	Swindon Borough Council
TD	Temple Mills (Stratford, London)	EWS
TE	Thornaby (Middlesbrough)	EWS
TH	Pershore Airfield, Throckmorton, Worcs	*Storage location only*
TJ	Tavistock Junction Yard	*Storage location only*
TM	Tyseley Locomotive Works	Birmingham Railway Museum
TO	Toton (Nottinghamshire)	EWS
TY	Tyne Yard (Newcastle)	EWS
WB	Wembley (London)	EWS
WD	Wimbledon (London)	South West Trains
WE	Willesden Brent Sidings	*Storage location only*
WI	Wilton (Teesside)	SembCorp Utilities
WS	West Somerset Railway (Minehead)	West Somerset Railway
YK	National Railway Museum (York)	Science Museum
YN	York Yard North, North Sidings	*Storage location only*
ZA	RTC Business Park (Derby)	Serco/AEA Technology/FM Rail
ZB	Doncaster Works	Wabtec
ZC	Crewe Works	Bombardier Transportation
ZD	Derby, Litchurch Lane Works	Bombardier Transportation
ZF	Doncaster Works	Bombardier Transportation
ZG	Eastleigh Works	Alstom UK
ZH	Springburn Works (Glasgow)	Alstom UK
ZI	Ilford Works	Bombardier Transportation
ZJ	Marcroft, Stoke	Turners
ZK	Kilmarnock Works	Hunslet-Barclay
ZN	Wolverton Works	Alstom UK
ZP	Horbury Works (Wakefield)	Bombardier Transportation

* = unofficial code.

ABBREVIATIONS

AFD	Air Force Department
C&W	Carriage & Wagon
DERA	Defence Evaluation & Research Agency
DSDC	Defence Storage & Distribution Centre
EY	Engineers' Yard

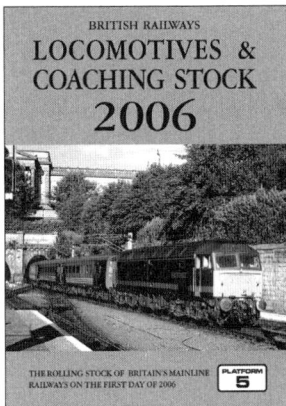